MULTI-DIMENSIONAL PROBLEMS OF WOMEN IN KASHMIR

MULTI-DIMENSIONAL PROBLEMS OF WOMEN IN KASHMIR

B. A. Dabla

GYAN

GYAN PUBLISHING HOUSE

NEW DELHI-110002

Multi-Dimensional Problems of Women in Kashmir

ISBN: 81-212-0923-4

Reprinted in 2012 in India by
Gyan Publishing House
23, Main Ansari Road, Daryaganj,
New Delhi - 110002
Phones : 23282060, 23261060
Fax : (011) 23285914
E-mail : books@gyanbooks.com
Website: gyanbooks.com

Printed at: G. Print Process, Delhi

Contents

Preface

It is generally believed by the experts that the life conditions among women in the Kashmir valley started undergoing change from the early decades of the present century. The factors responsible for this transformation included emerging political consciousness, expanding modern education, spreading cultural awareness, deteriorating economic conditions and large scale social awakening. Moreover, the political, economic and social developments in the Indian sub-continent had positive and necessary impact on the overall situation in Kashmir.

Mass change among women in Kashmir started from the early decades of the present century, especially from the early 1930s when the freedom movement started here. It was in the context of that movement that women in Kashmir were provided equal rights which were enshrined in the NAYA KASHMIR PROGRAMME that guided all post--independence governments in Jammu and Kashmir state. Thus the process of emancipation of women in Kashmir started with the initiation of the movement for political independence.

After 1947, when the local leadership assumed political power in the state after a long period of alien political domination, successive governments in the state attempted to improve the conditions of women. Many efforts in this direction were started. For example, free modern education, especially professional and technical education, was provided to the women from primary to university level. But, at the same time, the government programmes about the welfare of women were neither properly planned nor carried out with the degree of seriousness it deserved.

In the context of the above, the Kashmiri women in general faced many crucial problems in the fields of education, employment, health, hygiene, family, marriage, culture, diet and so on. These problems got expanded and intensified when the women started working outside their homes on regular and remunerative basis. In the past 10 years of militancy, the women's problems were multiplied. Consequently, the women in Kashmir got trapped in backwardness and degeneration. The processes of development and emancipation were restrained and had lesser effect on them.

Keeping in view the above mentioned social situation, women in general in the Kashmir valley faced tremendous problems inside as well as outside their homes. In actuality, various processes of social transformation were concomitantly followed by serious, basic and multi-dimensional problems among women in Kashmir.

It is important to note that these problems were multiplied and intensified during the last 10 years of militancy. The developments related to militancy, directly and indirectly, had negative impact on the processes of independence, development and overall emancipation of the Kashmiri women. They suffered, qualitatively as well as quantitatively, in all fields of life, especially education, employment, psychology, health, politics as so on. This situation has led to their backwardness in all crucial fields of life. In the prevailing situation, while the women in Kashmir have been trapped in this 'degenerative inferno', their backwardness may continue in the near future.

Thus there emerges a crucial and urgent need to arrest the women's degenerative and backward trends among women in Kashmir. The government and society at large have play their respective roles for the overall emancipation and total development of all women in Kashmir.

An important fact related to this situation is that the study of the problems of women become very difficult in the absence of relevant statistics. In actuality, there is a total dearth of the primary as well as of secondary source data. The immensity of these problems increased significantly because the decadel census in 1991 was not carried out in the state. Moreover, in the post-1991 census period, no official or unofficial survey/study was carried out by the government agencies/organizations.

It is essentially in this situational context that there emerges the highest degree of urgency and relevance for surveyor study like this one. That is also why we have added the report of another study entitled *Working Women in Unorganized Sector: A Socio-Economic Study in Kashmir.* This study too dealt specifically with the then emerging problems of the women working in the handicraft sector in the Kashmir valley.

Dr. Bashir A Dabla

Acknowledgements

First of all, I feel grateful to all concerned officials in the Ministry of Planning and Programme Implementation, New Delhi for financial sponsorship of the research project on the topic *Multi-dimensional Problems of Women in the Kashmir Valley*. Mr. Harish Chandra and Dr. R. N. Pandey, both Joint Directors in the Ministry of Statistics and Programme Implementation, New Delhi for their continued help and guidance at all stages of research for this survey. Dr. R.N. Pandey, who was the Monitoring Officer of this research Project, will be remembered by all of us here for his valuable supervision and professional guidance in this research project. His visit to the valley in the month of March 1999 proved highly encouraging and extremely useful for the entire team researchers. Mr. Chandra and Dr. Pandey deserve more thanks for their visit to the valley in very harsh weather conditions to participate in two-days workshop here in November 1999.

I am thankful to Mr. Riyaz Ahmad Mir, Project Co-ordinator, and all 24 Research Investigators for their hard and purposeful research work in the Valley. I was conscious on the fact that the prevailing situation in Kashmir was not completely normal and peaceful. In fact, their work in the field involved some degree of insecurity. But, despite all these odds, they carried out the field work with maximum degree of satisfaction. I will remember all these sincere efforts on the part of researchers. Mr. Mir deserves all appreciation for his hard work throughout the course of the project.

I may hardly forget the help and cooperation provided by the Resource Persons in the valley. Their role proved highly relevant. They include Professor A. G. Madhosh [Dean, Faculty of Education, University of Kashmir], Professor Raees Akhtar [Dean, Faculty of, Social Sciences, University of Kashmir], Professor Fayaz Ahmad [Dean, Faculty of Commerce and Management Studies, University of Kashmir] and Professor Dost. Mohammad [Head, Department of Economics, University of Kashmir]. I feel grateful to all of them.

I also thank the secretarial staff of the project, Mr. Gawhar Ahad and Ms. Nusrat Amin. They had to work hard even at odd hours.

The faculty members, research scholars, M. A. students and non-teaching staff of the .Department of Sociology, University of Kashmir, Srinagar provided help and cooperation at different stages of this research. I thank them all. Mr. Khurshid Ahmad, Statistician in Cent" for Population Studies, University of Kashmir helped in the statistical work related to the research project. I thank him too.

I appreciate the help provided by Computer Master, Srinagar in typing this manuscript neatly and in time.

At this stage, we must not forget the most important component of this research. That is the groups and sub-groups of 4,800 women respondents living in all six districts in the Kashmir valley. We "wasted" their precious time and often disturbed their daily work- schedule. But, they showed the highest degree of patience. I feel extremely thankful to all of them. In fact, this research was not. possible at all without their active help.

I thank the government of Jammu and Kashmir, particularly the Education Department, for providing [though very late] the necessary N.O.C.

At the end, I remember all discomforts and disturbances which my family members had to bear with me. I will remember their patience. I express may gratitude to my wife [Effat Bashir] and children [Ambareen Bashir and Shariq Bashir].

Last, but not the least, I feel grateful to Professor Abdul Wahid [Acting] Vice Chancellor, University of Kashmir, Srinagar for providing all necessary facilities for organizing the workshop and for attending the inaugural session of the workshop. I also remain grateful to Professor Agha Ashraf Ali who was the Chief Guest at the workshop and inaugurated the workshop. Deep-felt thanks are for Dr. R. N. Pandey and Mr. Harish Chandra, Joint Directors in the Ministry of Statistics and Programme Implementation, Government of India, New Delhi for attending two-days workshop in Srinagar in November 1999 [to represent the ministry] in cold weather conditions. I am also thankful to all Resource reasons who studied the Draft Report carefully, made serious academic reviews and discussed their related views in different sessions of the workshop. Thanks also go to my teacher colleagues, research scholars, students and non-teaching staff of my department for ,making the workshop a grand success.

Dr. Bashir Ahmad Dabla
Head
Department of Sociology & Social Work
University of Kashmir
Srinagar-190006, J & K

Summary of the Findings

1. Social Problems

1. The practice of dowry is in vogue in the Kashmir valley. The dowry is generally paid to the boy's family by the girl's family, primarily on the insistence/desire of the girls. Our investigation in this regard revealed the following response:

S.No	Dowry in vogue	Yes[%]	No[%]	Total[%]
1.	Family	62.08	37.92	100.00
2.	Class Group	55.89	44.10	100.00
3.	Community	57.12	42.87	100.00
4.	Area	64.53	34.47	100.00

2. The inquiry about the amount of dowry paid before and after the marriage revealed the following information:

S. No.	Amount of dowry	Paid by respondents [%]
1.	Rs. 20,001- and less	26.47
2.	Between 20,001 - 50,000	26.02

(Contd.)

(Contd. Table)

S. No.	*Amount of dowry*	*Paid by respondents [%]*
3.	Rs. 50,001 - and above	22.39
4.	N.A /N.R. [*]	25.10

* Not Applicable /No Response.

These variations can be co-related to the rich-poor and rural-urban differences.

3. The dowry items given by the bride's family to the groom's family included [priority-wise] gold items, cash, crockery, household items, land, furniture-furnishing, copper set, fridge, washing machine, colour television, VCP, tape-recorder, scooter, car and clothes.

4. Our research divulged that the *mahr* is paid by all grooms actually or notionally because it is compulsory religious obligation. While it was paid in full by 29.97 per cent respondents, it was paid in parts by 21.75 per cent respondents. At the same time, 19.77 per cent respondents paid it notionally which means deferring or remitting its payment. For 28.50 per cent respondents, this practice was not applicable.

5. According to our survey, the amount of *mahr* was fixed before or at the time of marriage as per the details given below:

S. No.	*Amount of mahr fixed*	*Number of Respondents [%]*
1.	Upto Rs. 5,000	38.66
2.	Rs. 5001-20000	17.91

(Contd.)

Contd. Table

S. No.	*Amount of mahr fixed*	*Number of Respondents [%]*
3.	Rs. 20,001-50,000	9.62
4.	Rs. 50,001-1,00,000	4.60
5.	Rs.1,00,001 and above	1.68
6.	N.A / N.R.	100.00

6. In general, people in Kashmir have not adopted the practice of polygamy except in some exceptional cases. In actually, this practice is generally considered undesirable. Our survey gave the information given below :

S.No.	*People with number of wives*	*Number of respondents [%]*
1.	People with 1 wife	66.10
2.	People with 2 wives	7.87
3.	People with 3 wives	0.39
4.	People with 4 wives	0.04
5.	N.A / N.R.	30.58

7. In the case of polygamous marriages, while 23.34 per cent wives lived in separate residences where they faced relatively lesser problems, 76.25 percent wives lived in residences where they faced relatively more problems

8. The divorce to women is not common in Kashmir. Actually, it is considered undesirable practice by huge majority of women as well as men. In this survey, 1.79 per cent respondents had faced divorce by their husbands, while 67.62 per cent respondents had not faced this situation. 30.58 per cent respondents belonged to the N.A./N.R. category.

9. 1.78 per cent and 1.37 per cent of the total women respondents had experienced the divorce in the case of their families and localities respectively. At the same time, 98.41 per cent and 98.62 per cent respondents in their families and localities respectively had no such experience at all. It follows that the practice of divorce in the Kashmir valley has remained negligible.

10. When the divorces are less, the chances of remarriage of divorcees are lesser. The survey revealed that while 1.02 per cent of the total divorced respondents had remarried, 0.77 per cent had not done so. 98.20 per cent respondents belonged to the N.A/N.R. category.

11. It revealed that while 16.41 per cent women respondents had received the share in their parental property, 55.08 per cent respondents had not got it. Those respondents who had received it had not got it in full and at one time. It was observed that those women who were denied their due share in their parental property generally belonged to poor families which could not afford to distribute their immovable property. The .survey also conveyed the rural-urban differences in. giving the property share in full to the women. However, it was found that more and more people are becoming aware about giving women their due share of parental property. In this section, 28.50 per cent respondents belonged to the N.A./N.R. category.

12. After the marriage, while majority of women respondents had established good relations with and within in-laws families, it was not possible for a minority of the cases. In this regard, the survey revealed that while 88.19 per cent women had established good relations with their husbands, it was not possible for 12.81 per cent women. Again, 74.76 per cent married women were in a position to develop the harmonious type of relationship with their fathers/mothers-in-law, the rest, i.e. 26.24 per cent, could not do this.

13. The survey divulged that while 12.16 per cent women respondents were beaten regularly by their husbands, 57.33 per cent women had no such experience in their homes. 28.50 per cent respondents preferred to keep mum in response to the query in this regard.

14. It was found that 65.77 per cent working women respondent were working in the governmental offices/ organizations and 34.22 per cent of them were working in the non-governmental offices/organizations. It was also found that the former group of women faced more problems in comparison with their counterparts in the latter group.

15. In the present-day situation, when women star working outside their homes on regular and remunerative basis, they develop a dual role for themselves. On being probed in this regard, while 58.68 per cent working women seemed conscious about it, 40.50 per cent of them were not conscious about it.

16. After the adoption of working role by women, they invited several crucial problems for themselves and for their families. One such problem was the childcare of children during the day [office] time. Our inquiry in this connection revealed the following institutions, agencies and individuals were taking care of children during the day time:

S.No.	Children taken care of by	Number [%]
1.	Husband's family	49.93
2.	Parents' family	35.36
3.	Servants/Maids	10.01
4.	Others	01.52
5.	N.A/N.R.	03.36

17. Another important implication of the adoption of working role by women was related to the socialization of their children. Our investigation in this area showed that 62.75 per cent of the working women felt this type of socialization as positive, while 31.05 per cent of them felt contrary. 6.21 per cent respondents didn't opine in this regard.

18. The other aspect of the impact of the adoption of dual role by working women was related to the social environment within their families. While 46.12 per cent women respondents referred to the increase in deviance among children, 29.38 per cent respondents reported decreasing social control. 24.48 per cent respondents pointed towards other social issues in this regard.

2. Economic Problems

1. The women respondents and their families were performing the economic activities as per following details:

S. NO	*Economic Occupational activities performed by the women respondents and their families*	*Number [%]*
1.	Agricultural activities	36.00
2.	Handicraft activities	18.06
3.	Small Business activities	07.77
4.	Household-Occupational	07.68
5	Other Economic activities	21.06

2. The survey found that new economic activities were started by the respondents in the fields of government service [55.69 per cent], non-government service [7.04 per cent], and horticulture [1.63 per cent].

3. The survey revealed that 54.65 per cent women respondents work on the agricultural land in rural areas. While 89.33 per cent of them work on their own land, 10.66 of them work on other's lands on share/wage basis. On the other hand, 45.31 per cent respondents didn't work on the agricultural land at all.

4. The investigation revealed that the wages [for working on other's lands) for women were considered "sufficient" by 7.14 per cent respondents, 72.85 per cent respondents considered these "not sufficient".

5. It was found that most of the women in the Kashmir valley work in different fields of the handicraft sector. They provide 30.52 per cent of their total work force in the fields of *Shawlbafi, kaleenbafi, shahtosh-phum weaving, paper-machine, wood-caving, crewel work and blanket weaving.* Majority of these women work in the fields of *shawlbafi* [37.40 per cent] and *kaleenbafi* [18.30 per cent). It was

observed that many girl children work in this sector, especially in the fields of *shawlbafi, paper-machine* and crewel work.

06. As is expected, the dominant majority of women workers, i.e. 84.57 per cent, were not getting due wages for their hard handicraft work, while 15.42 per cent respondents felt otherwise. Further inquiry in this area revealed that these wages fulfilled the basic needs of life in the case of 51.32 per cent respondents and not fulfilled in the case of 48.67 per cent respondents.

07. In the prevailing wage-worker scenario in the handicraft sector, there is a lot of scope for exploitation of the workers. Our inquiry in this regard divulged that while 84.57 per cent women workers felt that they were exploited systematically at the hands of middlemen, wholesalers and exporters, 15.42 per cent workers felt otherwise

08. The investigation showed that while 67.04 per cent working women respondents worked in the government offices, 32.95 per cent respondents worked in the non-governmental offices. Again the investigation showed that 48.03 per cent working women respondents' offices located in their own areas, while 51.96 per cent respondents' offices located in other areas.

09. The survey revealed that the working women respondents belonged to the salary categories as has been mentioned below:

S.No.	*Salary Category*	*Number of Respondents [%]*
1.	Up to Rs. 5,000/-	47.93
2.	Between Rs. 5,001 and Rs. 10,000	45.37
3.	Rs. 10,001/- and above	04.88

10. The regular salary of 72.49 per cent working women respondents had given them the required degree of economic independence in terms of earning as well as spending by themselves, while it has not happened in the case of 27.50 per cent respondents. It was observed that while 57.25 working women respondents spend their income themselves, 43.34 per cent respondents do not spend their income themselves. It was also observed that 57.14 per cent working women respondents spent their salary for their self needs only, while 42.86 per cent respondents spent for self and family needs.

11. In general, the women living in rural and urban areas performed the economic activities as mentioned below:

Rural Areas

S.No	*Economic sector*	*Number of respondents [%]*
1.	Agriculture	33.56
2.	Handicraft	21.68
3.	Harti-Flouriculture	09.66

Urban Areas

S.No	*Economic sector*	*Number of respondents [%]*
1.	Govt. service	10.89
2.	Non-Govt. service	05.60
3.	Handicraft	09.33
4.	N.A / N.R.	17.90

12. The exploitation of women workers in all sectors of economy goes on and increase day by day. Our probe in this regard revealed that 52.39 per cent respondents confirmed this, while 32.27 per cent respondents gave the opposite opinion.

13. All educated women in rural as well as in urban areas must get the government jobs necessarily. This opinion was held by 73.62 per cent respondents. On the other hand, 18.16 per cent respondents didn't agree with this opinion.

14. The government has started several programmes which are also aimed at the overall improvement in the conditions of women. These programmes include IRDP, TRYSEM, DWCRA, PRY, JRY and OAY. Our investigation revealed that only 17.63 per cent women respondents were benefited partly or wholly by these programmes. On the other hand, 77.29 per cent women respondents were not benefited by these programmes.

3. Educational Problems

01. The survey revealed that 29.50 per cent of women respondents were literate and 70.41 per cent were illiterate. These figures go in consonance with the estimates in early 1990s about female literacy in the Kashmir valley. However, there are inter-district differences in literacy rates which reflects in the following data collected in the survey:

S.No	*District*	*Literacy [%]*
1.	Anantnag	46.00
2.	Baramulla	22.00
3.	Budgam	18.75

(Contd.)

(Contd. Table)

S.No	District	Literacy [%]
4.	Kupwara	22.00
5.	Pulwama	12.50
6.	Srinagar	54.25

The qualification of the literate respondents was as follows:

S.No.	Qualification	Number of respondents [%]
1.	Primary	34.43
2.	Middle	21.80
3.	Matric	16.33
4.	Higher Secondary	12.46
5.	B.A/ B.Sc.	07.74
6.	M.A /M.Sc./ M.Com.	01.83
7.	Ph.D	00.35

2. The survey conveyed that the rate of literacy among members in the family, especially the girls, depends upon the literacy status of the elders, especially the parents/guardians. In this context, the literacy of the respondents can be inferred from the details given below:

S.No.	Elder Educated Persons in the Family of Parents	Number [%]
1.	Father	31.01
2.	Mother	15.79

(Contd.)

(Contd. Table)

3.	Brother/s	40.54
4.	Sister/s	27.93
5.	Others	32.22

3. More or less, the same response was received from the respondents vis-a-vis the literacy of elder members in the family of their husbands. The details in this regard follow:

S.No	*Elder Educated Persons in the Family of Husbands*	*Number [%}*
1.	Father-in-Law	25.50
2.	Mother-in-Law	12.81
3.	Brother-in-Law	27.70
4.	Sister-in-law	20.41
5.	Others	35.22
6.	N.A / N.R.	29.50

4. The inquiry revealed that in an average family [having 6.11 members on an average], there were 1.17 male and 1.26 female educated members. At the same time, there were 1.90 male and 1.78 female uneducated members in an average family.

5. The survey gave the information that 60.95 per cent women respondents felt there were sufficient educational facilities [such as school buildings, teachers, necessary equipment, libraries and laboratories] available in the schools. On the other hand, 30.14 per cent respondents conveyed that these educational facilities

were not available fully or were totally absent. 8.90 per cent respondents belonged to the N.A./N.R. category.

6. The investigation showed that, at present, 2.96 children on an average in a family go to the school. The sex ratio of these children is 1.71 boys and 1.24 girls. It follows that there prevails least discrimination against the female children at the elementary stage of school-going.

7. The number of drop-outs from the school stands high. While 21.00 per cent male children dropped from the school up to Matric stage, it was 22.33 per cent in the case of female children. However, these figures have to be seen in relation to much higher drop-out rates in the broader context.

8. The cost of education is high in Kashmir. It includes tuition fee, school dues, pocket money, transport charges, and other necessary expenditure. The survey divulged that 39.67 per cent respondents spent an amount up to Rs. 500/- per child per month on an average on the education of their children, while 27.22 per cent respondents spent an amount ranging between Rs. 501/- and Rs. 1,000/-- per child per month for the same purpose. Other 8.95 per cent respondents spent an amount of Rs. 1,000/- and above per child per month on the education of their children. The levels of this expenditure seem co-related with class affiliation of the parents.

9. The survey showed that while children of both sexes of 40.15 per cent respondents were studying in government schools, children of 30.47 per cent respondents were in the private-missionary schools. The studies in these different kinds of schools has necessary impact on the quality of education, expenditure on education and so on. 28.50 per cent respondents belonged to the N.A/N.R. category.

10. The survey conveyed widespread awareness among parents about the career-oriented education of their children. Thus 40.89 per cent parents strongly favored this type of education for their children. Moreover, majority of the respondents want to give their children professional-technical education. While 27.66 per cent respondents were not conscious about the importance of education, 28.50 per cent respondents belonged to the N.A/N.R. category.

11. The following languages were used as medium of instruction in the schools of the children of the respondents:

S.No.	*Language used as medium of instruction*	*Number of Respondents [%]*
1.	English	33.31
2.	Urdu	32.50
3.	Hindi	2.35
4.	Kashmiri	2.52
5.	N.A / N.R	29.33

4. Health Problems

1. Our survey investigation revealed that the health institutions and facilities in the valley are not available as per the needs in rural and urban areas. Significant number of such institutions and facilities, which were functioning/existing before 1990, were destroyed or closed during the last decade of militancy. So, the actual number of such institutions and facilities is not available.

2. The survey research conveyed that 58.43 per cent children of the respondents had undergone the process of immunization completely. They had taken the full course of BCG, OPT, Polio and Measles. On the other hand, 9.79 per cent children of the

respondents had taken immunization partly or not at all. This situation can be partly explained in terms of non-availability of these facilities and ignorance of the masses, and partly in terms of the militancy situation in the valley. Rest of the 28.50 per cent respondents belonged to the N.A./N.R. category.

3. The respondents identified four major/common diseases among their children and they were:

S.No	*Major/Common Diseases*	*Number of Respondents [%]*
1.	Cough and Cold	58.54
2.	Dysentery	61.70
3.	Usual Fever	41.00
4.	Jaundice	23.10

4. The survey revealed that 53.50 per cent respondents had taken the prenatal and post-natal care. While 78.52 per cent respondents had availed these facilities at the Public Health Centres in their areas of residence, 21.47 per cent respondents had gone to the Private Health centres. On the other hand, 15.75 per cent respondents had not taken pre and post-natal care at all. Rest of the 28.50 per cent respondents belonged to the N.A/N.R. category.

5. The survey found that the following persons conducted the delivery of the respondents or other persons in their families:

S.No.	*Delivery conducted by*	*Number of Respondents [%]*
1.	Doctor	20.66
2.	A.N.M	04.09
3.	Trained Dai	14.60

(Contd)

(Contd. Table)

S.No.	Delivery conducted by	Number of Respondents [%]
4.	Untrained Dai	14.60
5.	Relative	16.73
6.	Neighbour	09.10

6. The inquiry found that 20.66 per cent women respondents delivered their babies in the [government] hospital, 05.33 per cent respondents went to the Private Nursing Homes for the same purpose. However, majority of the cases, i.e. 74,00 per cent, were treated in their homes.

7. The research investigator gave the following information regarding the number of children born and died or survived:

S.No.	Number of children[average]	Total	Male	Female
1.	Born	3.5	1.7	1.7
2.	Living	2.8	1.4	1.3
3.	Dead	1.0	0.2	0.6

8. A dominant number of respondents, i.e. 63.39 per cent of the total, felt that they need no more children, male or female, while 4.10 per cent respondents felt the need to have more children. Those who conveyed the wish to have one more child numbered 60.19 per cent, 2 more children numbered 26.09 per cent and 3 more children 11.16 per cent. The response of the respondents had the particular sex bias. While 69.13 per cent respondents favoured to have male child/children, 30.76 per cent respondents favoured to have female child/children. The N.A/N.R. category composed of 28.50 per cent respondents.

9. Majority of the respondents were conscious about the ill effect of having more children. Thus 62.29 per cent respondents conveyed that more children will certainly face adverse effects on their health, while 8.83 per cent respondents gave the opposite response.The rest of 28.87 per cent respondents preferred to keep mum in this regard.

10. The survey revealed that the respondents responded to the illness differently. 07.14 per cent respondents go to the priest immediately after getting ill. Second, 42.29 per cent respondents go to the nearby medicine shop [a common practice in the Kashmir valley] and get the medicine on their own choice or at the advice of non-qualified and non-professional medical practitioner there. Third, 35.64 per cent respondents visit the local P.H.C. at the time of getting ill. Fourth, only 14.91 per cent respondents consult the expert doctor after they fall ill and get his advice for treatment. In these cases, the doctor charges the consultation fee.

11. The local P.H.C.s are attended rarely by the people. This reflects in the lesser visits to these centres by the people. The details follow:

S.No	*Visit to the local P.H.C*		*Number of Respondents [%]*
	Period	*Number of Times*	
1.	1 month	1	27.50
		2	14.64
		3	8.18
		None	49.62
2.	1 year	1-5	37.02
		6-10	32.37

(Contd)

(Contd. Table)

S.No	Visit to the local P.H.C		Number of Respondents [%]
	Period	**Number of Times**	
		11-15	8.27
		16 and more	6.55
		None	16.20

12. The breast feeding continues as a common practice. Thus 50.77 per cent married respondents breast feed their children, while 19.68 per cent respondents do not do it.

13. The investigation revealed that 88.18 per cent women respondents are fully aware about the benefits of the family planning programmes. On the other hand, 11.81 per cent respondents were not aware fully in this regard. The difference in awareness about family planning programmes was mainly because of education.

14. Our probe about the use of various family planning methods revealed the information mentioned below:

S.No.	Visit to the local P.H.C	Number of Respondents [%]
1.	I.U.D./C.U.T.	06.18
2.	Oral Pills	58.25
3.	Condoms	04.35
4.	N.A./N.R.	

5. Discrimination Problems

1. The working women are harassed continuously at their places of work. However, the occurence of this practice is very low here. While 22.17 per cent working women respondents maintained that they were harassed at their places of work, 79.82 per cent respondents have not faced this problem so far.

2. The harassment of women at their places of work was mainly of physical and mental nature. While 38.18 per cent working women respondents reported physical harassment, 34.14 per cent of their colleagues reported the mental torture in their offices. 10.85 per cent respondents registered other kinds of harassment in their offices.

3. While 46.28 per cent working women respondents felt that their harassment was carried out by their officers, 42.28 per cent respondents maintained that this practice was performed by other [equal or senior] colleagues. 11.42 per cent respondents held that the harassment of women colleagues in their offices can be carried out by any colleague of their's, senior, junior or equal.

4. The research investigation found that while 1.14 per cent working women respondents registered their complaint with the officers concerned against their harassment, 82.85 per cent respondents had not done *so.* 16.00 per cent respondents preferred to remain silent about this question. Those who complained against their harassment got the following result:

- satisfactory	50.00 per cent respondents
- not satisfactory	50.00 per cent respondents

Those who didn't complain against their harassment gave the reasons mentioned below:

- don't want to highlight their harassment	55.17 per cent respondents
- to avoid negative social reaction	22.75 per cent respondents
- to avoid discrimination in the office	25.51 per cent respondents

5. It was found that 29.15 per cent respondents mainly working in the handicraft sector were getting lesser wages than their male counterparts. On the other hand, 70.84 per cent female

respondents were getting equal wages for their work. It was reported that 52.17 per cent respondents had complained to the concerned against lesser wages, but their response was not satisfactory.

6. In a specific investigation in the handicraft sector, it revealed that 53.00 per cent women workers were discriminated in the payment of wages, while 46.96 per cent respondents were not discriminated.

7. In the field of inheritance rights, while 43.37 per cent women respondents were given these rights fully, 36.75 per cent respondents were not given these rights. 19.87 per cent respondents belonged to the N.A/N.R. category. In the cases of 21.29 per cent respondents, religion was made the basis for denial of these rights, while as religion grants these rights of women. That is what is the opinion of 62.16 per cent women respondents.

8. The majority of 63.16 per cent women respondents felt that there' exists no law which discriminate or hurt the interests of women. On the other hand, 14.64 per cent women respondents opined that some laws discriminate women, 22.19 per cent respondents preferred to be silent on this topic.

9. The survey revealed that women respondents had lesser authority than men. This reflected clearly in the authority pattern related to control over property, daily decision-making, marriage of children, money investment, children's education, and construction of new house.

10. In the on-going process of discrimination, the girl child gets discriminated more than others. While 60.43 per cent women respondents agreed on this statement, 28.31 per cent respondents disagreed. 11.25 per cent respondents remained silent in this regard.

11. The survey revealed that 18.14 per cent women respondents were in favour of abortion, especially when the baby is female. But, at the same time, 41.16 per cent respondents were absolutely opposite to the practice. 49.16 per cent respondents did not opine on this crucial issue.

1

Introduction

1. Women in the Global Context

1. The sociological investigation of the human society at the global level has revealed that women in general in the distant and recent past faced unfair and unequal treatment at the hands of their own and other men. Their role in totality was characterized with dependency, inferiority and acute suffering. They lived like somebodys property. In actuality, they have faced systematic discrimination; institutionalized suppression and multi-dimensional exploitation. The historical records of the human past reveals that this situation related to women prevailed more or less in all human societies situated in all continents. This situation also prevailed irrespective of human societies' differences in race, region, religion, economy, social structure, culture, and in other fields of life. These sociological propositions about the status and role of women in the traditional societies are not mere theoretical or ideological abstractions but essentially stand for the empirical social reality of the human past. It may be argued that while some human societies practised highest degree of negative attitude and behaviour towards women, other societies had adopted lowest degree in this regard.

2 However, the fact of contemporary importance stands that women at the global level and in continuity have undergone wider and deeper processes of transformation in the earlier and current centuries. While women in the European and American continents have undergone radical transformation in the previous few centuries, women in the Asian, African and Latin American continents faced certain degree of change in the present century. This multi-farious change among women in the developed as well as developing countries had complete or partial effect on the traditional status and role of women in these societies. This large-scale, deep-rooped and multi-faceted change among women can primarily be related to the short-term and long-term implications of the processes of modernization, especially development and change. While change refers to the processes of industrialization, urbanization, demographic transformation, secularization, adoption of science and technology in day-to-day life, scientific temper, modern education, materialistic worldview and so on, development points toward improvement in overall conditions of life, especially increase in income, literacy, exposure, improvement in health-nutrition and total advancement in personality and societal traits.

3. It was in the context of preceding social dynamics that women started undergoing basic change and consequently developing new role and status for themselves as well as for the entire womenfolk. The conditions of women in India must essentially be seen in this background.

2. Women in India

1. Like the women in other Asian and African societies, women in India in the past were trapped in a traditional situation which was characternized by discrimination, suppression,

inequalityand other features. The Hindu caste system and its implications had made the condition of women worse and they were not allowed to challenge the then existing situation. However, the change among women here could neither be stopped nor resisted. Consequently, women in the broader Indian society experienced significant degree of change in many fields of life, especially education, employment, health and nutrition.

2. This process of women's emancipation in India was accelerated in the post--independence era. The governments in India, in respective of their political and ideological a1fferences, pursued the grand objective of women's betterment in totality. This objective was made an important part of the national planning and development processes. Successive development plans, at the central as well as at the state level, initiated several programmes and schemes for women's betterment.

3. On the other hand, many voluntary agencies and organizations, which emerged in India in the recent decades, played a significant and effective role in the overall betterment of women here. They worked consistently and systematically to improve general conditions of women in rural and urban India. It has been observed that these NGOs' efforts have proved highly useful in individual and group cases. They proved more successful because of women's confidence in them and their acceptability among women.

4. As a result of serious efforts on the part of GOs and NGOs in the post-dependence period, the conditions of women in every part-region of India have improved significantly, though not satisfactorily. This present situation is characterized with three main feature.

First, the change in the position of Indian women has penetrated all communities, groups and regions. The view upheld by some that women of some communities/ groups/regions have not been touched by the general improvement in the status is not correct. In actuality, women of all communities in India have responded positively to the processes of change in varying degrees. This change may be lesser quantitatively, but it stands significant in the relative context. The sociological investigations of women in many parts/states of India, belonging to the minority community of Muslims, have revealed that they have accepted and adopted change in their attitudes and behaviour. In some fields, they have marched ahead of the women of other communities in India.

Second, change among women in India has to be seen in a contextual form. It implies that this change is neither consistent nor logical completely. There has not emerged inevitable relationship between change in one field of life and the other. For example, no necessary correspondence has developed between changes at the ideational and behavioural levels among women. Other studies have revealed that women had undergone a considerable degree of mobility in the economic field but it was not followed, correspondingly and necessarily, by mobility in the social and other fields.

Third, women belonging to varying groups and classes and different communities have not responded to the processes of change in the same way, interest, vigour and intensity. As is the case with natural dynamics, different ethnic, religious and regional groups/ communities have responded to the processes of change differently.

3. Women in Kashmir

1. In the traditional Kashmiri society, women generally remained confined to or around the family. Their world of activities was, confined within the borders of their parti-local household. While not considered equal inside as well as outside their families, they were usually subjugated, abused, discriminated and mal-treated in the social life. They could not develop their individual personality or be independent from the males. Actually, they remained dependent on fathers/male guardians, as wives on their husbands, and as mothers on their males throughout their lives. As daughters, they remained dependent on their sons. This life cycle of female dependency was supported by the culture and religion. This dependence was so deep-rooted that even the personal matters of women in the family were decided by the eldest male members. Their income was usually considered the family's income and was often received as well as spent by the males. It is important to note here that majority of women in the valley were economically productive mainly due to the nature of economic activities here. Most of traditional economic sectors/fields were directly or indirectly related to the world-famous Kashmiri handicrafts. The women here in rural and urban areas composed the major part of workers in these sectors/fields. It is estimated that more than 50 per cent of workers in the handicraft sector/fields are women.

2. The complete domination of men over women crudely reflected in the mal- treatment which the latter got at the hands of the former. The women, especially wives, were beaten in some families and there was no collective protest against this brutal practice. Though some individual protests were observed, but these were insignificant and ineffective. Consequently, the practice of wife-beating was considered 'undesirable normal practice' in

the family context. Moreover, the women in large numbers were not allowed even to participate in the decision-making process. In actually, all important decisions related to all matters, including decisions about women, were the exclusive prerogative of elder male members of the family. Women were not allowed even to participate in the deliberations regarding decisions.

3. Women in the traditional Kashmiri society were considered unequal, inferior and weak mentally and physically. These notions were supported by myths, dogmas and traditional belief system. Many women too believed strongly in these men-created notions and ideas, which had a strong impact on the behaviour of women in the entire life. However, strict adherence to the practice of endogamy kept the women here in close contact with their parental/ paternal families. This type of relationship between families put a serious restraint on bad treatment of women at the hands of their husbands and their families.

4. Though Islam allowed the practice of polygamy with certain conditions and limitations, it was never common among the Muslims in Kashmir. The practice was socially insignificant and was generally considered 'undesirable' because of its abuse by some individuals. Moreover, factors like meagre income, underlying feeling that justice cannot be done to two or more wives at a time, and the constant tension in the family reduced further the occurrence of polygamy. The general argument presented was that if you cannot do justice to more than one wife, you should/must not marry second/ third/fourth women. No statistical figures are available about the number of polygamous marriages in the valley. However, experts in Kashmir feel that its number was very less. While three or four wives type of marriages were non-existent, two wives type of

marriage had some occurrence. The latter type of marriage was done because of the death or ill-health of the first wife or her insterility.

5. Similarly, the practice of divorce, religiously allowed with certain obligations on the part of the husband, was not common in the valley. No official or unofficial figures are available in this regard. The concerned experts here feel that divorces were rare in the valley and this number was socially negligible. This situation may be explained by factors like close relations between families, fear of retaliation of divorce from the other side and strong social pressure against divorce.

6. The Islamic *Shariah* allowed the Muslim women to inherit a particular share from the property of their parents and husbands. Though these inheritance rights for women in the valley existed in theory, these were denied to them in practice. In actuality, a customary law was developed which did not allow a due share to women from their parental property. Again, though the *mehr* stood as a legal right [the payment of which must be made before the finalization of marriage], it was usually denied to them in part or full in practice.

7. In reality, the women in Kashmir in the past were caught in a paradoxical situation. While their social role was projected as minimal, they participated actively in social, economic and other activities. In urban areas, while the women of *sayyid* and *hojja* families were confined completely to their homes and *were* not allowed to perform any manual labour outside their homes, women belonging to various occupational groups and communities worked with their men both within and outside their homes for earning

sufficient amount of money required to fulfill the family needs. In the rural areas, all women worked side by side with their male family members in the agricultural fields.

8. The women in Kashmir generally did not practise *purdah* which meant the wearing of the formal *Burqa* from head to toe. This practice applied to all groups of the Kashmiri society except the *Sayyid* and hojja women. These two groups practised various forms of *purdah* due to religious and social reasons.

9. Generally, there prevailed no segregation between women and men in the traditional society of Kashmir. The interaction between the opposite sexes usually took place at all levels, in all fields and in all sections of society. In fact, the institutional arrangement in the occupations in the valley was developed in such a way that the male-female interaction, both with insiders and outsiders, seemed must.

4. Change among Women in Kashmir

1. The situation of women explained above prevailed for centuries in the Kashmir valley and has been recorded by some historians, missionaries, tourists and travellers. It is generally believed by the experts that conditions in Kashmir in general and the Kashmiri women in particular started undergoing change from the early decades of the 20th century. Two major sets of factors are mainly responsible for the initiation of this broader and deeper change. First, at the endogenous level, emerging political consciousness, expanding modern education, spreading of cultural awareness, deteriorating economic conditions and large-scale social awakening created a situation in which women felt concerned

about their position. They also started thinking about their rights in the broader social context. Second, at the exogenous level, there was a strong impact of the process of *neubremization* which refers to a process of impact of the outside developments on the inhabitants in the valley. Accordingly, all political, social, economic and other developments in the Indian sub-continent, especially erstwhile United Punjab and Delhi, had necessary impact on overall situation in the Kashmir valley. Interaction with and exposure to the outsiders/aliens made adoption of change easy, contextual and relevant.

2. Mass change among women in Kashmir started from early decades of the present century, especially from early 1930s when the freedom movement started in the state. The women in the valley in general participated in that movement against the feudal rule of the *Maharaja* dynasty in large numbers and their men put no restriction on them. That was the first time in Kashmir history when women in large numbers came out of their homes and participated in a social-political movement. It was essentially in the context of .that movement that women in Kashmir [and in the state of Jammu and Kashmir at large] were provided equal rights [to men's rights] which were enshrined in the Naya Kashmir Programme in 1938 that guided all post-independence period governments in J and K state. In that changing context, while the *sayyid-hojja* women responded early and fully to the changing processes, other women, belonging to lower socio-economic groups/classes responded to change very late.

3. After 1947, when the local political leadership assumed political power, successive governments in J&K state, irrespective of political and ideological differences, attempted to improve the conditions of women here. Many efforts in this direction were started. Free education, including technical and professional education,

was provided to the women from primary to the university level. Women were assured jobs in government offices, technical - professional institutes, public and .private enterprises and commercial business establishments. The government also safeguarded political, economic and social rights of women. However, it was observed that these programmes for women's welfare were neither properly planned not carried out with commitment and seriousness. The political instability in the state in the entire post-1947 period was mainly responsible for this situation.

4. In the post-independence decades in J&K state, three major developments related to women took place. These development were:

First, there emerged a mass consciousness among women [and other members of society too] about their rights within as well as outside their homes. This had a qualitative impact on the family life, especially in relation to the status and role of women.

Second, the Kashmiri women in general and belonging to all classes, groups and communities achieved a fair degree of social and cultural mobility which also helped in the fast breakdown of the institutional structure of the traditional family. In this situational context; women felt relatively easy to deviate from the traditional practices and enlarge their role.

Third, most important, the Kashmiri women at large developed motivation and interest in coming out of their homes for various purposes like education, employment and entertainment. As a result of this development, many women were recruited in various employment sectors. In actuality, there emerged a general pattern in rural as well as urban areas according to which all educated girls sought education, and subsequently, employment necessarily.

5. It is important to note here that the above-mentioned changes among women were directed towards their change and development. In totality, these changes contributed step-by-step to their emancipation. However, these changes were associated with other problems for women and their family members. Prominent among these problems include problems of child-bearing and child-rearing, their undesirable socialization and uncontrolled behaviour, women's dual role and post-marital conflict/mal adjustment and their discrimination and harassment in out-home situations. It follows that women in the traditional Kashmiri society faced one set of problems such as total dependence on men, lower social status, confining their role to their homes, imposition of ideas and behaviour related to the women. Now, in the changing situation, women faced another set of problems which included women's dual role, child-bearing and child-rearing problems, and marital disharmony. In this situation, the women's problems became complex and their complexity increases day-by-day. Moreover, the short-term and long-term implications of these problems are completely undesirable for women and the society at large.

6. The problems of women in the Kashmir valley are multifarious and are felt in every field of life. However, we have identified five sets of primary and crucial problems of women, the details of which follow:

[i] Social Problems

- practice of dowry
- non-payment of *mahr*
- status of wife
- practice of polygamy

- divorce to women
- remarriage of divorcees and widows
- denial of women's share in the parental property
- post-marital relations
- practice of wife-beating
- undesirable places of work
- dual role working women
- problems of child care
- undesirable socializaticn of children
- family disorganization and its implications

[ii] Economic Problems

- pattern of traditional occupations and women's participation
- occupational mobility and women
- women's work on agricultural land
- payment of wages to women workers
- women workers in the handicraft sector
- exploitation of women workers
- women's work outside their homes
- regular salary and economic independence of women
- pattern of spending by working women
- economic activities performed by women
- educated women and government jobs
- women benefited by governmental programmes.

[iii] Educational Problems

- literacy among women
- educated persons in the families of parents and husbands
- availability of educational facilities
- school-going children in the family
- drop outs from the school

- cost of education of children
- career-oriented education for women

[iv] Health Problems

- health institutions and facilities available
- immunization of children
- common diseases among children and their mothers pre-natal and post-natal care
- conduct and place of delivery.
- number of children of women
- effects of having more children
- response to the illness by women
- visit to the local P. H.C.
- breast feeding of children
- awareness about family planning

[v] Discrimination Problems

- harassment of working women
- discrimination in the wage payment
- complaint against lesser wages
- discrimination of women in handicraft sector
- discrimination of women in inheritance rights
- religion and discrimination against women
- authority pattern of women
- discrimination against girl child
- abortion of female fetus by women

It is in the above thematic framework that we have focussed on the women in Kashmir to know their multi-dimensional problems. As the existing situation reveals these dimensions of women's problems represent their basic, crucial and central problems. In actuality, these various problems portray the totality of women's problems.

2

Methodology

1. Theoretical-Empirical Framework

At the initial stage, a realistic understanding and broader perspective about various existing problems of Women in the Kashmir valley was developed from the available primary and secondary sources. These sources include documents such as Ph.D. Thesis [published and unpublished], books, journals, newspapers, magazines, reports, files, personal documents and so on. The available necessary data on the concerned theme/s was also collected.

Subsequently, wider empirical investigation about the topics was carried out through a sample survey among the respondents belonging to different classes, groups and communities. In fact, all findings in this survey are specifically based on the field investigation carried out by research investigators in all districts of the Kashmir province of Jammu and Kashmir state. Thus the propositions developed on the basis of investigation are empirical realities.

2. Sample of the Survey

The sample of the survey was of the representative type. A serious attempt was made to give representation to all relevant variables such as demography, age, sex, education, income, social status, marital status, language, and religion. All these variables were selected consciously in order [a] to give due representation to all concerned groups and sub-groups in the sample, and [b] to get the maximum required information/data on specific themes/ topics. All these details about the sample of survey reveal in the following table :

Table 1
STATUS OF RESPONDENTS IN THE FAMILY

S.No	*Theme/Question*	*Respondents [district-wise]*						*Total*
	Are you the Head	*A*	*B*	*B*	*K*	*P*	*S*	
	of Family	*No./%*	*No./%*	*No./%*	*No./%*	*No./%*	*No./%*	*No./%*
1.	Yes	50	70	-	110	-	10	240
		6.25	8.75	-	13.75	-	1.25	30.00
2.	No	750	730	800	690	800	790	4560
		93.75	91.25	100.00	86.25	100.00	98.75	70.00
	Total	800	800	800	800	800	800	4800
		100.00	100.00	100.00	100.00	100.00	100.00	100.00

* A for Anantnag B for Baramulla B for Budgam
K for Kupwara P for Pulwama S for Srinagar

Table 2
AGE GROUP OF THE RESPONDENTS

S.No	Theme/Question	Respondents [district-wise]						Total
	Are groups of the Respondents	A	B	B	K	P	S	
		No./%	No./%	No./%	No./%	No./%	No./%	No./%
1.	11-20 years	320 40.00	270 30.75	310 38.75	316 39.56	340 42.50	276 34.50	1832 38.16
2.	21-35 years	200 25.00	210 26.25	270 33.75	300 37.50	290 30.00	270 33.75	1540 32.16
3.	36-50 years	200 25.00	230 28.75	210 26.25	170 21.25	150 18.75	240 30.00	1200 25.00
4.	51 years & above	80 10.00	90 11.25	10 1.25	14 1.75	20 2.50	14 1.75	228 4.75
	Total	800 100.00	800 100.00	800 100.00	800 100.00	800 100.00	800 100.00	4800 100.00

Table 3
MARITAL STATUS OF THE RESPONDENTS

S.No	Theme/Question	Respondents [district-wise]						Total
	Marital status of the Respondents	A	B	B	K	P	S	
		No./%	No./%	No./%	No./%	No./%	No./%	No./%
1.	Married	518 64.75	542 61.75	544 68.00	572 7.15	650 81.25	481 60.12	3307 68.89

(contd.)

(contd.Table.3)

S.No	Theme/Question	Respondents [district-wise]						Total
	Marital status of the	A	B	B	K	P	S	
	Respondents	No./%	No./%	No./%	No./%	No./%	No./%	No./%
2.	Unmarried	267	238	240	200	133	290	1368
		33.37	29.75	30.00	25.00	16.62	36.25	28.50
3.	Divorced	9	15	10	20	12	20	86
		1.25	1.87	1.25	2.50	1.50	.50	1.79
4.	Separated	3	5	2	5	3	6	24
		0.37	0.62	0.25	0.62	0.37	0.75	0.50
5.	Widow	3	-	4	3	2	3	15
		0.37	-	0.50	0.37	0.25	0.37	0.31
	Total	800	800	800	800	800	800	4800
		100.00	100.00	100.00	100.00	100.00	100.00	100.00

Table 4
INCOME GROUPS OF THE RESPONDENTS

S.No	Theme/Question	Respondents [district-wise]						Total
	Income groups of the	A	B	B	K	P	S	
	Respondents[per month]	No./%	No./%	No./%	No./%	No./%	No./%	No./%
1.	Up to Rs.2000/-	210	300	290	380	290	100	1570
		26.25	37.50	36.25	47.50	36.25	12.50	32.70
2.	Rs.2001-4000/-	340	280	285	200	300	250	1655
		42.50	35.00	35.62	25.00	37.50	31.25	34.40

(Contd.)

(Contd. Table 4)

S.No	*Theme/Question*	*Respondents [district-wise]*						*Total*
	Marital status of the	*A*	*B*	*B*	*K*	*P*	*S*	
	Respondents	*No./%*	*No./%*	*No./%*	*No./%*	*No./%*	*No./%*	*No./%*
3.	Rs.4001-6000/-	151	161	166	160	157	300	1089
		18.87	20.12	2.75	30.00	18.87	37.50	22.65
4.	Rs.6001-8000/-	71	30	20	40	15	110	236
		8.87	3.75	2.50	5.00	1.87	11.75	5.95
5.	Rs.8001-10000/-	20	15	25	15	39	39	14.4
6.	Rs.10001/-& above	8	14	4	5	5	10	56
		1.00	1.5	1.75	0.62	0.2	1.25	1.16
	Total	800	800	800	800	800	800	4800
		100.00	100.00	100.00	100.00	100.00	100.00	100.00

Table 5
LITERACY AMONG THE RESPONDENTS

S.No	*Theme/Question*	*Respondents [district-wise]*						*Total*
	Literate / Illiterate	*A*	*B*	*B*	*K*	*P*	*S*	
		No./%	*No./%*	*No./%*	*No./%*	*No./%*	*No./%*	*No./%*
1.	Illiterate	432	624	650	624	700	350	3380
		54.00	78.00	81.25	78.00	87.50	43.75	70.58
2.	Literate	368	176	150	176	100	450	1470
		44.00	22.00	18.75	23.00	12.50	56.25	29.58

(Contd.)

(Contd Table 5)

S.No	Theme/Question	Respondents [district-wise]						Total
	Literate / Illiterate	A	B	B	K	P	S	
		No./%	No./%	No./%	No./%	No./%	No./%	No./%
3.	Qualification:							
	-Primary	109	57	30	60	32	201	489
		29.61	32.38	20.00	34.09	32.00	44.66	34.43
	-Middle	90	38	40	35	35	100	338
		24.45	31.54	20.66	19.08	35.00	23.72	23.07
	-B.A/B.Sc.	85	38	45	41	18	60	287
		23.09	21.58	29.99	23.19	18.00	13.33	20.21
	-M.A/M.Sc.	10	5	2	1	3	5	26
		2.71	2.84	1.33	0.56	3.00	1.11	1.83
	-Doctorate	2	1	-	-	-	2	5
		0.54	0.52	-	-	-	0.44	0.10
	-Prof./Tech.	15	3	3	15	2	12	50
		4.06	1.68	2.66	6.43	2.00	2.66	1.04

Table 6
RELIGION OF THE RESPONDENTS

S.No	Theme/Question	Respondents [district-wise]						Total
	Religion of the	A	B	B	K	P	S	
	Respondents	No./%	No./%	No./%	No./%	No./%	No./%	No./%
1.	Hinduism	20	15	10	5	25	10	85
		2..50	1.87	1.25	0.62	3.12	1.25	1.77

(Contd.)

(Contd Table 6)

S.No	Theme/Question	Respondents [district-wise]						Total
	Literate / Illiterate	A	B	B	K	P	S	
		No./%	No./%	No./%	No./%	No./%	No./%	No./%
2.	Islam	740	750	765	785	750	740	4530
		92.50	93.75	95.62	98.15	93.75	92.50	94.37
3	Sikhism	30	30	20	10	25	50	165
		3.75	3.75	2.50	1.25	3.12	6.5	3.43
4.	Christianity	10	5	5	-	-	-	20
		1.25	0.62	0.62	-	-	-	0.41
	Total	800	800	800	800	800	800	4800
		100.00	100.00	100.00	100.00	100.00	100.00	100.00

Table 7
OCCUPATIONS OF RESPONDENTS FAMILIES

S.No	Theme/Question	Respondents [district-wise]						Total
	Occupation of	A	B	B	K	P	S	
	Respondents families	No./%	No./%	No./%	No./%	No./%	No./%	No./%
1.	Agriculture	300	350	290	450	355	100	1845
		37.50	43.75	36.25	58.05	44.37	2.50	38.43
2.	Handicrafts	233	230	310	170	225	210	1378
		29.12	28.75	38.75	21.25	28.12	26.25	28.70

(Contd.)

(Contd. Table 7)

S.No	Theme/Question	Respondents [district-wise]						Total
	Occupation of	A	B	B	K	P	S	
	Respondents families	No./%	No./%	No./%	No./%	No./%	No./%	No./%
3.	Govt.Service	150	162	140	125	159	450	1186
		18.75	20.25	17.50	15.62	19.87	56.25	24.70
4.	Business	80	48	30	35	51	30	274
		10.00	6.00	3.75	4.37	6.37	3.75	5.70
5.	Small-scale industry	37	10	30	20	10	10	117
		4.62	1.25	3.75	2.50	1.25	1.25	2.43
	Total	800	800	800	800	800	800	4800
		100.00	100.00	100.00	100.00	100.00	100.00	100.00

Table 8
TYPES/MEMBERS OF FAMILY OF RESPONDENTS

S.No	Theme/Question	Respondents [district-wise]						Total
	Structure of the	A	B	B	K	P	S	
	Family	No./%	No./%	No./%	No./%	No./%	No./%	No./%
1.	Joint Family	300	410	385	420	405	320	2240
		32.50	51.25	48.12	52.50	50.62	40.00	46.66
2.	Nuclear Family	500	390	415	380	395	480	2560
		62.50	48.75	51.87	77.50	49.37	60.00	53.33
3.	No.of members:Total	6.4	6	6.8	5	6	6.4	6.11

(Contd.)

(Contd. Table 8.)

S.No	Theme/Question	Respondents [district-wise]						Total
	Structure of the Family	A	B	B	K	P	S	
		No./%	No./%	No./%	No./%	No./%	No./%	No./%
	-Males	3	3	3.8	3	4	3.2	3.33
	-Female	3.4	3	3	2	3.2	2.78	2.78
	-Major	4	2	2	3	2.5	2.4	2.65
	-Minor	2.4	-	4.8	2	3.5	4	3.46
	-Earning	4	2	2.8	3	2.5	2.4	2.68
	-Non-Earning	2.4	4	4	2	3.5	4	3.33

Table 9
MOTHER TONGUE OF THE RESPONDENTS

S.No	Theme/Question	Respondents [district-wise]						Total
	Mother Tongu of the Respondents	A	B	B	K	P	S	
		No./%	No./%	No./%	No./%	No./%	No./%	No./%
1.	Kashmiri	740	700	760	780	25	5	3010
		92.50	87.50	95.00	97.50	3.12	0.62	62.70
2.	Urdu	00	50	5	5	750	700	1550
		00	6.25	0.62	0.62	93.75	92.50	32.29
3.	Hindi	20	15	10	5	-	00	50
		2.50	1.87	1.25	0.62	-	-	1.04

(Contd)

(Contd. Table 9)

S.No	Theme/Question	Respondents [district-wise]						Total
	Mother Tongue of the respondents	A	B	B	K	P	S	
		No./%	No./%	No./%	No./%	No./%	No./%	No./%
4.	English	10	5	5	-	-	-	20
		1.25	0.62	0.62	-	-	-	0.41
5.	Others	30	30	20	10	25	55	170
		3075	3.75	2.50	1.25	3.12	6.87	3.54
	Total	800	800	800	800	800	800	4800
		100.00	100.00	100.00	100.00	100.00	100.00	100.00

Table 10
PLACES OF RESIDENCE OF THE RESPONDENTS

S.No	Theme/Question	Respondents [district-wise]						Total
	Places of residence of the respondents	A	B	B	K	P	S	
		No./%	No./%	No./%	No./%	No./%	No./%	No./%
1.	Urban area	200	190	230	160	185	610	1575
		25.00	23.75	28.75	20.00	23.00	76.25	32.81
2.	Rural area	600	610	570	640	615	190	3225
		75.00	76.25	71.25	80.00	76.87	23.75	67.18
	Total	800	800	800	800	800	800	4800
		100.00	100.00	100.00	100.00	100.00	100.00	100.00

3. Universe / Area of survey

This survey specifically concentrated on the women respondents living in the Kashmir valley, i.e. the Kashmir province in the Jammu and Kashmir state. This province is composed of six following districts:

a) Anantnag
b) Baramulla
c) Budgam
d) Pulwama
e) Kupwara
f) Srinagar

In order to make the sample highly representative, all districts, tehsils and blocks in the valley were give due representation. Every sub-unit too was made representative. Thus the total unit of survey was the women society in the valley.

4. Methods and Techniques Adopted

The relevant data/information about the concerned topic was collected from the women respondents through a detailed questionnaire. This questionnaire was distributed among the literate respondents who filled these either themselves or with the help of research investigators. However, the questionnaire-based interviews were conducted by the investigators among the illiterate and semiliterate respondents. This proved highly relevant and accurate. Other formal steps, like the adoption of Kashmiri language in the conversation with the respondents, were taken to record the respondents responses correctly and properly. For motivating the respondents, especially in the urban areas, some gift pieces were offered to them. That solved the problem of rapport-making partly on the one hand; and helped getting the correct information on the other.

5. The Questionnaire

The questionnaire for this survey was of the stratified type. It composed of the thematic and problem-oriented questions. These were of the fixed-choice as well as open-choice questions about the nature, dimensions, causes, consequences and other related aspects of the topic of problems of women in Kashmir. All questions were oriented to collect maximum statistical information. The questionnaire of 1991 census related to women, with certain additions and deletions, was also incorporated within the thematic framework of this questionnaire. It may not be out of place to mention here that the draft of questionnaire was adopted after getting it approved by the Ministry of Statistics and Programme Implementation. Finally, the questionnaire was composed of six sets of questions each dealing with a specific theme. While the first set composed of questions dealing with biographical details of all respondents, the other five sets dealt with the following themes:

[a] Social Problems;
[b] Economic Problems;
[c] Educational Problems;
[e] Health Problems; and
[f] Problems of Discrimination.

6. Recruitment and Training of Research Investigators

After the proper advertisement in the local dailies, the posts of Project Co-ordinator [01], Research Investigators [24] @ of 04 per district and Secretarial Assistant [02] were selected through format interviews as per the Kashmir University rules. The minimum qualification for Project Co-ordinator and Research Investigators was M.A. in Sociology or allied subject such as Social Work. Subsequently, the necessary training to the project Co-ordinator and Research Investigators was provided for 3-4 weeks time by the Resource Persons and other experts in the concerned field. The themes of the training revolved around the scientific method and its application in the field and questionnaire and interview methods. The investigators were fully trained in recording the response of the respondents and made them aware about the possible problems. In this way, these qualified investigators were exposed to the entire process of investigation.

7. Fieldwork

All persons, Project Director, Project Co-ordinator and Research Investigators, carried out the fieldwork for a period of 3-4 months. It started in December 1998 and ended in March 1999.

The fieldwork for the survey was carried out in all six districts in the Kashmir valley with some difficulties in some areas. It was ensured that all rural and urban areas are covered in the investigation. In order to follow this aim, all tehsils and blocks in all districts were covered necessarily. However, some areas were land-locked at that time because of heavy snowfall in winter there. The areas of Gureg and Karnah in Baramulla district are such areas. In these areas, the fieldwork was carried out in March, 1999 when these became accessible. Though the research investigators faced a lot of problems, they carried out the required fieldwork satisfactorily.

8. Data Processing

After all fieldwork was over, the process of checking and counter-checking was carried out by the Project Co-ordinator and the Project Director. In this work, all mistakes, wrong and incorrect contents were removed.

Subsequently, the data aggregation was done on the basis of themes and sub-themes. At this stage, the repetition and duplication of data, if any, was removed. It was done jointly by the research investigators and the statisticians. All this work was done manually by the research investigators.

This was followed by the tabulation of statistics collected in the fieldwork. This was specifically done as per the questions and sub-questions in the questionnaire. This work enabled us to the formulation of the theme-based tables in all chapters.

In the final stage of data processing, the data was described/ explained according to the needs and objectives of the survey.

9. Major Field Problem

Several problems were faced by the research team members, especially the research investigators, during the course of investigation. First, the most serious problem which the team faced in all districts was related to the safety and security. Since the conditions of militancy prevail in all districts, except the Srinagar district, the research team members are followed/watched and [in some cases] harassed. Two of our research investigators in Kupwara and Baramulla were taken by the militants. But, after long interrogation, they were freed without any torture. In fact, we resolved this problem by sending the research investigators to their own district/tehsil/block of residence. Since people [and the local militants too] knew them, they were not touched.

Second, since some areas in the valley remain cut off during the winter months due to heavy snowfall, we could not approach the respondents at that time. However, we were in a position to contact them in March 1999. Thus our work got delayed by one month, which was conveyed to the ministry in due time.

Third, the Kashmir valley generally experience the heavy snowfall during the winter season. In that situation, the entire valley remains cut off from the outside world. Even the contact between several areas, all within the valley, becomes impossible. Our research team too faced these problems. But, the facilities provided by us negated many such problems. It may not be out of place to mention here that the team of researchers worked during the winter months in minus degree temperatures, varying from -1 to -8.

Fourth, as per the instructions of the Ministry of Statistics, we had to get the N.O.C. from the J & K state government before starting the work. But, the state government was so apathetic that a simple NOC took me 4-5 months. Consequently, we got delayed by about 5 months in starting the work on research project.

Fifth, several problems, such as problems related to transport, power curtailment, and non-availability of experts, were faced by the team.

10. Workshop and Revision

After Draft Report of the survey was submitted in the ministry, it suggested the organization of a workshop in Srinagar to have a critical review and objective assessment of the findings of the survey carried out in the valley. In order to make it a standard practice, copies of the Draft Report were provided to all Resource Persons to prepare their reviews. Subsequently, the two-days workshop was organized in Srinagar in November 1999. The critical reviews were presented in different sessions of the workshop and thus findings of the survey were reviewed fully and discussed/debated extensively by the participants. The two- days deliberations in the workshop led to the formulation of relevant suggestions. These suggestions were incorporation in the text and thus the revision of the Draft Report was carried out.

3

Social Problems

3.1. The practice of dowry

The practice of dowry is certainly in vogue in the Kashmir valley but in a different way. It may be explained in the way that there is no specific demand of dowry on the part of the boy or boy's family. But, the girls in dominant majority cases ask [in some cases compel] their parents to give them a lot of things [details of these things explained in the following tables] which they take to the boy's house after marriage. The girls' parents give these things to their daughters happily considering [these things] as dowry. Our investigation regarding this theme gave us the response entered in the following table:

Table 1
THE PRACTICE OF DOWRY

S.No	*Theme/Question*		*Respondents [district-wise]*						*Total*
	Is the practice of Dowry in vogue?	*Posi./ Nega.*	*A*	*B*	*B*	*K*	*P*	*S**	
			No./%	*No./%*	*No./%*	*No./%*	*No./%*	*No./%*	*No./%*
1.	Family	Yes	400 50.00	758 94.75	400 50.00	122 15.25	500 62.50	800 100.00	2980 62.08

(Contd.)

(Contd. Table 1)

S.No.	Theme/Question	Posi./ Nega.	A No./%	B No./%	B No./%	K No./%	P No./%	S* No./%	Total No./%
	Is the practice of Dowry in vogue?								
		No	400	42	400	678	300	-	1820
			50.00	5.25	50.00	84.75	37.50	-	37.92
2.	Class/Group	Yes	300	752	400	131	300	800	2683
			37.50	94.00	50.00	16.37	37.50	100.00	55.89
		No	500	48	400	669	500	-	2117
			62.50	06.00	50.00	83.62	62.50	-	44.10
3.	Community	Yes	313	742	373	154	410	750	2742
			39.12	92.7	46.62	19.25	51.25	93.75	57.12
		No	487	58	427	646	390	50	2058
			60.68	7.25	53.37	80.75	48.75	6.25	42.87
4.	Area	Yes	378	736	700	141	390	800	3145
			47.25	92.00	87.50	17.62	48.75	100.00	42.87
		No	422	64	100	659	410	-	1655
			52.78	8.00	12.50	82.38	51.25	-	34.47

*A= Anantnag B= Baramulla B= Budgam
K= Kupwara K= Pulwama S= Srinagar

The table reveals that the practice of the payment of dowry from the girl's family to the boy's family at the time of marriage stands existing in a significant way. This applies to all situations related to his family, class/group, community and area of residence. Thus 62.08 per cent, 55.89 per cent, 57.12 per cent and 65.52 per cent respondents showed this response vis-a.-vis their families, class/groups, communities and areas respectively. Though the trend of dowry exists in all areas, it stands more in the urban areas than the rural areas. The table shows that, in Srinagar district, all 800 respondents [i.e. 100.00 per cent] agreed with this proposition. The respondents in other districts, all rural dominated, didn't agree with such proportion. It is important to know that the response of "no" does not convey that they don't pay the dowry at the time of marriage of their daughters or take it at the time of marriage of their sons. It conveys that they have not paid dowry on demand from the boy's side or they pay lesser/insignificant amount of dowry.

3.2. The Amount of Dowry Paid

It is generally believed that the amount of dowry paid to the boy's family by girl's family at the time of marriage is not same. It varies from family to family and group to group. In fact, the amount of dowry is paid/determined by the economic and social standing of the family concerned. Moreover, there prevails regional differences in the patterns of dowry. Our investigation in this regard gave us information included in the following table 2:

The table 2 reveals that majority of respondents belonged to two categories which paid less than Rs. 20,000/- or amount between Rs. 20,001 and 50,000/- as dowry for themselves or for their family members. The respective proportion in these categories is 26.47 per cent and 26.02 per cent. While the former respondents [1271/4800. i.e. 26.47 per cent] generally belong to lower classes/groups of occupational workers, lower salaried employees, petty businessmen and so on, the later respondents,

[1249/4800, i.e. 26.02 per cent] compose of the groups such as professionals. technicians, experts, middle-upper salaried employees and small businessmen.

Table 2
THE AMOUNT OF DOWRY PAID

S.No	Theme/Question	Respondents [district-wise]						Total
	Amount of dowry	A	B	B	K	P	S	
		No./%	No./%	No./%	No./%	No./%	No./%	No./%
1.	Rs. 20,000/-& less	328	224	350	73	360	100	1271
		41.00	28.60	43.75	9.12	45.00	12.50	26.47
2.	Rs. 20,001-50000	248	368	260	47	250	200	1249
		31.00	46.00	30.50	5.87	31.75	25.00	26.02
3.	Rs. 50,001 & above	152	176	100	33	140	500	1075
		19.00	22.00	12.50	4.12	23.35	62.50	22.39
4.	N.A/N.R.*	72	32	90	647	50	-	1205
		9.00	4.00	11.25	80.87	6.25	-	25.10
	Total	800	800	800	800	800	800	4800
		100.00	100.00	100.00	100.00	100.00	100.00	100.00

* N.A/N.R. = Not Applicable/ No Response

The Table 2 also reveals the regional variation in the amount of dowry. While People living in urban areas pay relatively higher amount of dowry in comparison to their counterparts living in rural areas. In our study, 500[i.e. 62.58 per cent] respondents in the Srinagar district paid dowry worth Rs. 50,000/- and above. But, the respondents in other districts could not match this figure. Again,

100 per cent respondents in Srinagar district showed their responses, while respondents in other districts didn't show their responses fully.

3.3. Variety of Dowry Items

It is well known that there exist variety of items of dowry, which are taken from the girl's home to the boy's home after marriage among all classes, groups and communities. The basis for this variety are provided by the cultural-religious context, social-economic standing and regional differentiation. In the Kashmir valley, certain special and general items are sent from the girl's home to the boy's home before and at the time of marriage. These items are similar as well as dissimilar with the items which are used as dowry items outside Kashmir. These items in the Kashmir valley can be divided in two major parts. First, the items of daily use such as car, television, furniture-furnishing and fridge. Second, the items of occasional use such as golden jewellery, crockery and land.

In the above thematic context, we asked the respondents to identify major items of dowry in their areas priority-wise. The items which they mentioned were rated in terms of the responses. These rated responses have been shown in figure 1 which follows:

3.4. *Mahr* fixed at the time of marriage

The *mahr* stands as the religious obligation and legal requirement for a Muslim at the time of marriage. According to the Islamic *Sharia,* the Muslim bridegroom is required to fix and pay fully the amount of *mahr* to the bride before the finalization of his marriage *[nikah].* The amount of *mahr* is fixed on the economic

Figure 3.1
Variety of Dowry Items

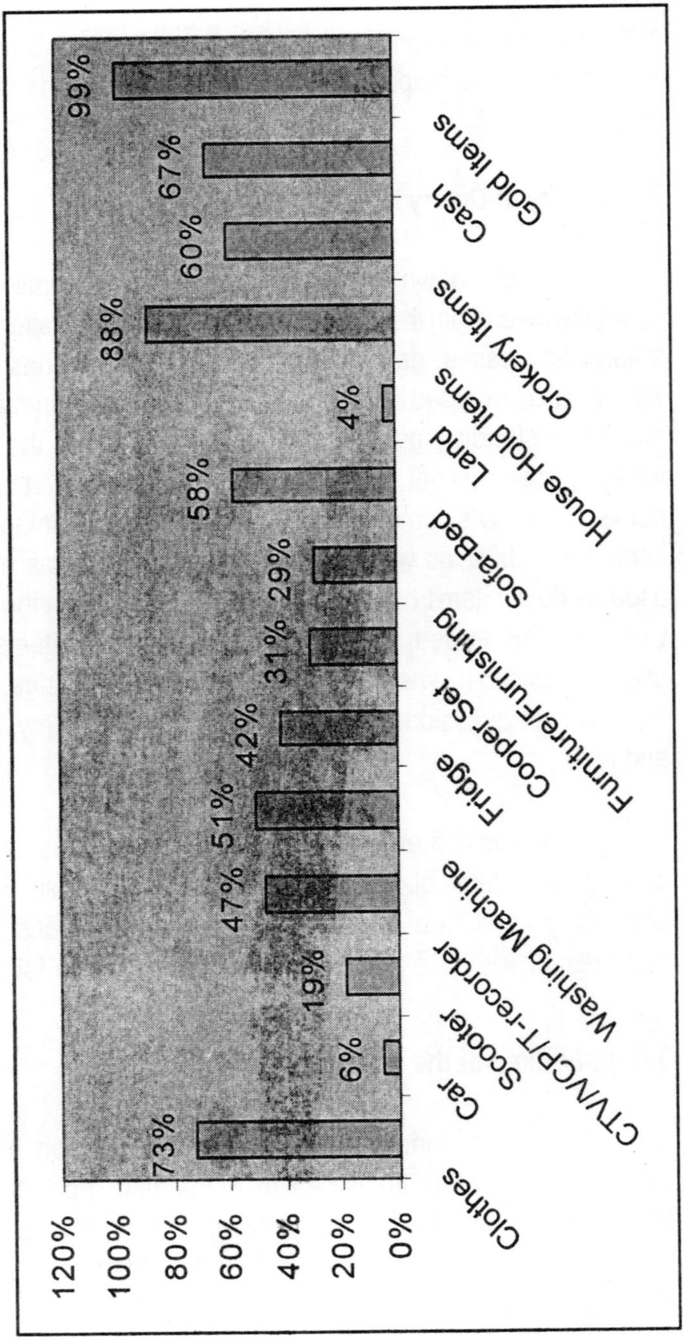

standing of the groom. The *mahr* is neither a bride price nor an economic security. In reality and totality, it is a fundamental religious obligation on the part of man to establish stable and durable relationship with women for the whole life. This relationship goes beyond the material dimensions and involves non-material aspects of life.

However, the fact stands that the amount of *mahr* is fixed and paid before the finalization of marriage *[nikah]* contract, on which both boy and girl agree. If the *nikah* ceremony is held before the day of marriage, then the amount of *mahr* fixed and paid also on that day. The Islamic *sharia* directs that the amount of *mahr* must be determined according to the economic standing, which can be measured in terms of income of the boy concerned, i.e. the bridegroom. The sharia-directed practice goes on in the Muslim society, though with some minor deviation. In the preceding religious-social context, our investigation in the relevant area got the response noted in the Table 3.

Table 3
MAHR FIXE AT THE TIME OF MARRIAGE

S.No	*Theme/Question*	*Respondents [district-wise]*						*Total*
	Amount of mahr fixed	*A*	*B*	*B*	*K*	*P*	*S*	
	at the time of marriage	*No./%*	*No./%*	*No./%*	*No./%*	*No./%*	*No./%*	*No./%*
1.	Up to Rs.5,000/-	398	357	390	310	300	101	1856
		49.75	44.62	40.75	38.25	37.50	12.62	38.66
2.	Rs.5,001-20,000/-	59	166	100	99	245	191	860
		7.37	20.75	12.50	12.30	30.62	23.87	17.91

(Contd.)

(Contd. Table 3)

S.No	Theme/Question	Respondents [district-wise]						Total
	Amount of mahr fixed	A	B	B	K	P	S	
	at the time of marriage	No./%	No./%	No./%	No./%	No./%	No./%	No./%
3.	Rs.20,001-50,000/-	37	45	50	125	55	150	462
		4.62	5.62	6.28	15.62	6.87	18.75	9.62
4.	Rs.50,001-100,000/-	19	26	10	66	50	50	221
		2.37	3.25	1.25	8.35	6.25	6.25	4.60
5.	Rs.100,001 & above	20	16	10	00	17	18	81
		2.50	2.00	1.25	00	2.12	2.35	4.68
6.	N.A./N.R.	267	190	240	200	133	290	1320
		33.37	23.75	30.00	25.00	6.62	36.25	27.50
	Total	800	800	800	800	800	800	4800
		100.00	100.00	100.00	100.00	100.00	100.00	100.00

The Table 3 conveys that all respondents, poor and rich, rural and urban, determined the amount of *mahr* at the time of marriage or signing of *nikah-nama.* A significant number of 1835/ 4800 [38.66 per cent] respondents fixed an amount upto Rs.5,000/ as *mahr*. These respondents belonged mainly to the lower classes and occupational groups, whose income is meager. The middle class groups [such as salaried employees, small businessmen, professionals and others] fixed the amount of *mahr* on the following pattern:

(a) Rs. 5,001 - 20,000	17.91 per cent
(b) Rs. 20,001 - 50,000	9.62 per cent
(c) Rs. 50,001 - 100,000	4.60 per cent

Only 81/4800 [1.68 per cent] respondents fixed the *mahr* of Rs. 1,00,000/- and above. The respondents belonged mainly to big business families, top bureaucrats politicians and so on.

3.5. Payment of *Mahr*

The general practice in the Kashmiri society seems that the amount of *mahr* is fixed after a long discussion between the parties concerned by all but not paid by all. Those who pay, many of them do not pay fully. Others defer the payment in full or part in order to avoid total payment. Though this goes against the directions of Islamic law, it happens continuously. Consequently, the women emerge as the sufferer. Our investigation in this field gave us the information noted in the Table 4.

Table 4
PAYMENT OF MAHR TO THE WOMEN

S.No	Theme/Question	Respondents [district-wise]						Total
	Payment of mahr	A	B	B	K	P	S	
		No./%	No./%	No./%	No./%	No./%	No./%	No./%
1.	Yes – full	147	251	270	310	231	222	1439
		42.36	32.37	33.75	38.75	28.87	27.25	29.97
	- part	57	170	131	150	190	203	1044
		57.3	21.25	16.37	18.75	23.35	35.37	21.75
2.	No.	186	133	154	140	246	85	949
		23.25	14.62	19.87	17.50	30.75	10.62	19.77

(Contd.)

(Contd. Table 4)

S.No	Theme/Question	Respondents [district-wise]						Total
	Payment of mahr	A	B	B	K	P	S	
		No./%	No./%	No./%	No./%	No./%	No./%	No./%
6.	N.A.N.R.	267	190	240	200	133	290	1320
		33.37	23.75	30.00	25.00	6.62	36.25	27.50
	Total	800	800	800	800	800	800	4800
		100.00	100.00	100.00	100.00	100.00	100.00	100.00

The Table 4 reveals clearly that majority of the respondents or their families, i.e. 51.72 per cent, had paid the amount of *mahr* to the bride at the time of marriage or when the *nikah* was finalised. It also reveals from the table statistics that while 29.97 per cent respondents had paid the amount of *mahr* in full, 21.75 per cent respondents had made the payment partly. In actuality, the latter respondents had deferred the payment of the part of *mahr* amount to future. This amount, according to the respondents, was never paid to women in future nor they demanded it from their husbands. In some cases only, women demanded this amount from men after their divorce took place.

On the other hand, 19.77 per cent respondents reported tha they were not paid the amount of *mahr* fixed and noted in th *nikah-nama*. In actuality, these respondents include those wome who were not paid fully. Thus a significant proportion of Musli women here suffer because of non-payment or part-payment mahr. This behaviour on the part of men can be related to thre major reasons. First, some men are economically so weak th they were not in a position to pay the amount of *mahr* fully at a tim

Second, there prevails ignorance among some men about the importance of the payment of *mahr* fully at the time of marriage. Third, some men consciously avoid the payment of *mahr* fully to their women and thus violate the religious injunction. It seems important to note here that it was observed that while the number of those who pay *mahr* fully is increasing, the number of those who avoid to pay *mahr* fully in decreasing.

3.6. Status of Wife

The practice of polygamy has been allowed not ordered in the Islamic religion with certain conditions and in certain situations. Though this practice is allowed among the Kashmiris living in the valley, it, at the same time, is considered extremely undesirable. Consequently, not many people in the valley marry more than one woman and keep more than one wife at a time. These views got confirmed in our investigation in the valley. The following Table 5 reveals it clearly:

Table 5
STATUS OF WIFE

S.No	*Theme/Question*	*Respondents [district-wise]*						*Total*
	Status of Wife	*A*	*B*	*B*	*K*	*P*	*S*	
		No./%	*No./%*	*No./%*	*No./%*	*No./%*	*No./%*	*No./%*
1.	First wife	517	506	510	80	50	500	3173
		64.62	63.25	63.75	72.05	70.00	63.50	66.10
2	Second wife	12	56	45	10	5	10	138
		1.50	7.00	5.62	1.25	0.60	1.25	7.87

(Contd.)

(Contd. Table 5)

S.No	Theme/Question	Respondents [district-wise]						Total
	Status of Wife	A	B	B	K	P	S	
		No./%	No./%	No./%	No./%	No./%	No./%	No./%
3.	Third wife	4	-	5	8	25	-	19
		0.50	-	0.62	1.00	0.25	-	0.39
4.	Fourth wife	-	-	-	2	-	-	2
		-	-	-	0.25	-	-	0.04
6.	N.A./N.R.	267	235	240	200	233	290	1468
		33.37	27.75	30.00	25.00	29.12	36.25	30.58
	Total	800	800	800	800	800	800	4800
		100.00	100.00	100.00	100.00	100.00	100.00	100.00

The statistics in the Table 6 reveals that the dominant majority of women respondents, i.e. 3173/4800 [66.10 per cent]. had the status of the first and the only wife.This goes in consonance with the general observation that people in Kashmir have not adopted the practice of polygamy except in some particular cases. The table also reveals that there were very insignificant cases of marriage with more than one woman, especially third and fourth. The details in this regard are:

- 138/4800 [7.87 per cent] respondents had 2 wives,
- 19/4800 [0.39 per cent] respondents had 3 wives,
- 02/4800 [0.04 per cent] respondents had 4 wives.

The reasons for these types of marriage, cited by respondents, included compulsion on the part of husbands especially when they get no child/children from the list wives. In general, it follows that, in Kashmir, though the polygamous marriage is not a taboo, but its practice stands uncommon and exceptional. It also reveals that the occurrence of polygamous marriages is more in the rural areas in comparison with the urban areas. Moreover, there are some family traditions in the hilly areas which contribute to the polygamous marriages.

3.7. Nature of Residence of Wives

After the polygamous marriage, the husband has to live in nuclear or joint family with all his wives. Two patterns have been observed in this regard. First, the husband establishes one or more than one nuclear family unit/s and live there with his wives. Second, the husband lives with all his wives in the joint family. In. all such situations, all women suffer more or less, especially in terms of lower social status, little inheritance rights and perpetual conflict and jealousy between the wives. Our inquiry about the residence of wives gave the following information:

Table 6
STATUS OF WIFE

S.No	*Theme/Question*	*Respondents [district-wise]*						*Total*
	Pattern of residence of wives	*A*	*B*	*B*	*K*	*P*	*S*	
		No./%	*No./%*	*No./%*	*No./%*	*No./%*	*No./%*	*No./%*
1.	Separate residence	101 18.94	195 34.87	111 19.82	138 23.00	85 12.74	185 36.27	815 23.34
2.	Joint residence	432 81.05	367 65.30	449 80.11	462 77.00	582 87.2	325 63.72	2617 76.25
	Total	533 100.00	562 100.00	560 100.00	600 100.00	667 100.00	572 100.00	3432 100.00

The above table reveals that about 24 per cent respondents live in separate households which their husbands established after first or second marriage. On the other hand, about 76 per cent respondents lived in the traditional joint households. As revealed in the previous table, the joint residences dominates the nuclear residence of wives. It also follows that while joint residence of wives takes place more in rural areas, nuclear residence is established in the urban areas. The table shows figures in this regard.

3.7. Polygamy-related Problems of Women

When women marry and become the second, third or fourth wife, she invites a lot of problems for herself and for her family. In reality, these women invite two sets of problems after the polygamous marriage. First, she faces all problems which every woman faces after marriage. Second, she invites additional problems due to the polygamous marriage. That is why the woman who becomes second or third wife has some serious limitation which compels her to go for this type of marriage.

When we probed about these problems. the women identified a series of problems because of polygamous marriage. All identified problems were rated and the results are shown in the Figure 3.2.

3.8. Divorce to the Women Respondents

The most crucial problem which the women face in the post-marriage situation is the divorce declared by the husband. This threat remains in the minds of women through out their life.

Figure 3.2
Polygamy Related Problem of Women

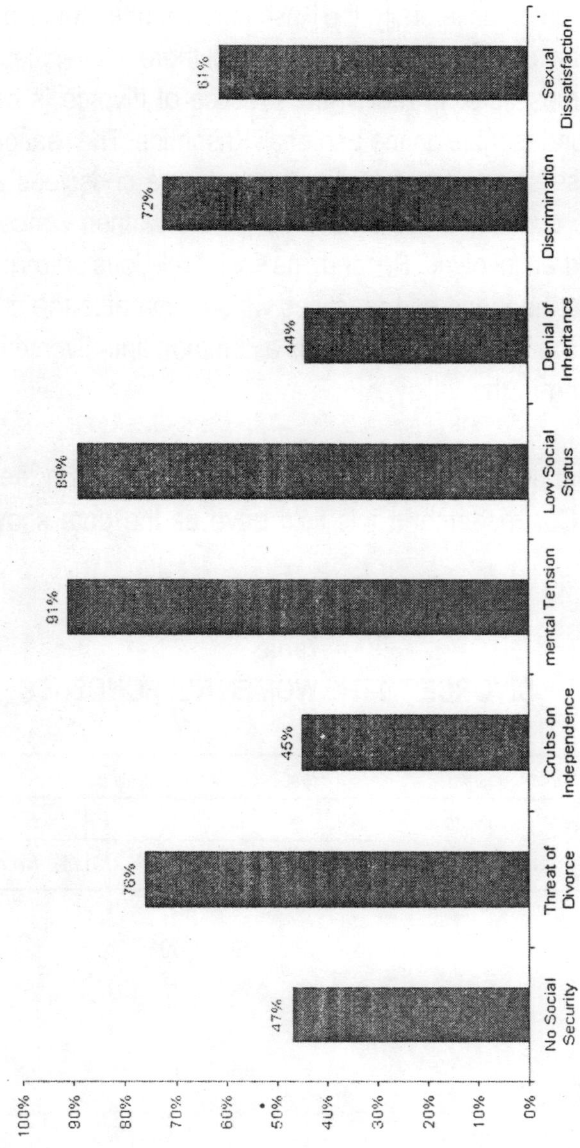

In comparison to other societies/communities in the Indian sub-continent, the occurrence of divorce is least. Since Islam has allowed with certain restrictions the practice of divorce by the man to the women unilaterally, the Kashmiris like other Muslims practice it too. But, our observation conveys that there are very less number of divorces here. In reality, the practice of divorce is considered highly undesirable on the part of all Kashmiris. The reasons for this response seems two-fold. First, people are conscious about the horrible consequences of divorce for the women concerned and the children involved. Second, the social-religious ethos of Kashmir negates the ideas and practices which separates the couple and breaks the family. It fact, there is a common anti-divorce sentiment prevailing in the valley.

But, in spite of all this, some divorces occur in the Kashmir valley. Our research in this field gave us the data shown in the Table 7.

Table 7
DIVORCE TO THE WOMEN RESPONDENTS

S.No	*Theme/Question*	*Respondents [district-wise]*						*Total*
	Were you divorced	*A*	*B*	*B*	*K*	*P*	*S*	
	By your husband?	*No./%*	*No./%*	*No./%*	*No./%*	*No./%*	*No./%*	*No./%*
1.	Yes	9 1.12	15 1.87	10 0.25	20 2.50	12 6.50	20 2.0	86 1.79
2.	No	524 65.50	57 69.40	550 68.75	580 72.25	555 67.37	490 61.25	3246 67.62

(Contd.)

(Contd. Table 7)

S.No	Theme/Question	Respondents [district-wise]						Total
	Were you divorced	A	B	B	K	P	S	
	By your husband?	No./%	No./%	No./%	No./%	No./%	No./%	No./%
3.	N.A/N.R.	267	138	240	200	237	290	1468
		33.37	29.75	30.00	25.00	29.12	61.25	30.58
	Total	800	800	800	800	800	800	4800
		100.00	100.00	100.00	100.00	100.00	100.00	100.00

The Table 8 conveys the response like the response of preceding table in which women had not faced this situation. It conveys that though the concept and practice of divorce is in vogue in the Kashmir valley, its occurrence stands ignorable and insignificant.This has been possible because of the domination of religious ethos, common anti-divorce sentiment and emancipation of women here. It was also found that some of the divorces, especially to the younger ones, remarried on the insistence of the family members and other relatives.

Table 8
DIVORCE TO OTHER WOMEN

S.No	Theme/Question	Respondents [district-wise]						Total
	Have you experienced	A	B	B	K	P	S	
	Divorce in your.....	No./%	No./%	No./%	No./%	No./%	No./%	No./%
1.	Yes-Family	15	7	10	10	12	20	76
		1.97	1.12	1.25	1.50	1.50	2.50	1.59
	-Locality	8	9	12	8	2	20	66
		1.00	1.12	1.50	1.00	0.25	2.50	1.37

(Contd.)

(Contd. Table 8)

S.No	Theme/Question	Respondents [district-wise]						Total
	Have you experienced	A	B	B	K	P	S	
	Divorce in your.....	No./%	No./%	No./%	No./%	No./%	No./%	No./%
2.	No- Family	785	793	790	790	788	780	4724
		98.30	99.17	98.75	98.75	98.50	97.50	98.41
	-Locality	792	793	788	792	798	780	4734
		98.92	98.88	98.50	99.00	99.75	97.50	98.62
	Total	800	800	800	800	800	800	4800
		100.00	100.00	100.00	100.00	100.00	100.00	100.00

However, this situation related to divorce is fast changing mainly as a result of the implications of the processes of modernization. We also inquired from the respondents about the situation related to divorce in their families and localities. More or less the same situation [reflected in the preceding table] prevailed there. The table gives details in the regard:

3.9. Remarriage of Divorcees

As was mentioned in the previous sections, some of divorcees marry again. In fact,remarriage is not a taboo but, at the same time, is not a desirable trait. Some women who feel compelled due to different factors remarry. In actuality, in the Kashmir valley, less number of women are divorced and lesser number of divorcees got remarried. In this background, we investigated about the phenomenon of remarriage of divorced women. The response we got has been incorporated in the Table 9.

Table 9
REMARRIAGE OF THE DIVORCEES

S.No	Theme/Question	Respondents [district-wise]						Total
	Remarriage of divorcees	A	B	B	K	P	S	
	[in last 1 year]	No./%	No./%	No./%	No./%	No./%	No./%	No./%
1.	Yes	4 0.50	5 0.2	10 1.25	10 1.25	10 1.25	10 1.25	49 1.02
2.	No	5 0.62	10 1.25	00 00	10 1.25	2 0.25	10 1.25	37 0.77
3.	N.A/N.R.	791 97.87	785 98.12	790 98.75	700 97.50	788 98.50	780 97.50	4714 98.20
	Total	800 100.00	800 100.00	800 100.00	800 100.00	800 100.00	800 100.00	4800 100.00

The statistics in the above table reveals clearly that a very less number of divorcees got remarried in the period of last one year. Their number was 49/4800 [1.02 per cent] which is very insignificant by any standard. It was observed during the investigation that these remarriages were carried out mainly due to the pressure of parents and relatives on the concerned women. It was also considered necessary to remarry the divorcees if they were young.

3.10. Women's Share in their Parental Property

One of the crucial problems women face in the period after marriage is related to the inheritance rights in their parental property. It is because they are denied to inherit their parental property partly or wholly, though Islam has given them a specific share in this property. Though this practice was in vogue at large, especially in the rural areas, it has reduced its effect in the present day context. We carried out detailed investigation in this regard. The response we got from the women respondents has been noted in the Table 10.

Table 10
WOMEN'S SHARE IN THEIR PARENTAL PROPERTY

S.No	*Theme/Question*	*Respondents [district-wise]*						*Total*
	Did you get the share	*A*	*B*	*B*	*K*	*P*	*S*	
	In parental property?	*No./%*	*No./%*	*No./%*	*No./%*	*No./%*	*No./%*	*No./%*
1.	Yes	110	52	200	235	101	100	788
		13.75	6.50	25.00	26.12	12.62	12.50	16.41
2.	No	423	570	360	375	566	410	2644
		52.87	63.75	45.00	46.87	70.75	57.25	55.08
3.	N.A/N.R.	267	238	240	200	133	290	1368
		32.00	29.75	30.00	25.00	16.62	36.25	28.50
	Total	800	800	800	800	800	800	4800
		100.00	100.00	100.00	100.00	100.00	100.00	100.00

The Table 10 conveys that while 788/4800 [16.41 per cent] women respondents had received their share in the parental property, 2644/4800 [55.08 per cent] respondents had not received that share. It follows that the majority of women in Kashmir are not still getting their share in the parental property. During the investigation, it was revealed that those women who get the share in parental property have not got it fully. Moreover, this share in many cases was not paid at a time but in installments. On the other hand, the parents of those women respondents who didn't get the share in parental property, belonged to poor classes and groups and were not able to give the share to their daughters. We also made an inquiry about major reasons responsible for non-payment of share to daughters. The rated response was as follows:

(a) meagre immovable property	80 - 90 per cent
(b) no need for daughters	70 - 80 per cent
(c) no tradition	60 - 70 per cent
(d) no demand by daughters	50 - 60 per cent

3.11. Amount of Share of Parental Property

As stands clear from the preceding Table 10, 788/4800 [16.41 per cent] women' respondents got the share from the parental property. We further investigated about the proper share and got the following response:

Table 11
AMOUNT OF SHARE IN PARENTAL PROPERTY

S.No	*Theme/Question*	*Respondents [district-wise]*						*Total*
	How much share in	*A*	*B*	*B*	*K*	*P*	*S*	
	Parental prop. you got?	*No./%*	*No./%*	*No./%*	*No./%*	*No./%*	*No./%*	*No./%*
1.	01-50 per cent	488	500	510	490	490	250	2728
		61.92	64.10	64.72	62.18	62.18	31.72	-
2.	50-100 per cent	300	388	378	398	399	538	2401
		38.08	35.90	35.28	38.82	38.82	68.28	-

(Contd.)

(Contd. Table 11)

S.No	*Theme/Question*	*Respondents [district-wise]*						*Total*
	How much share in	*A*	*B*	*B*	*K*	*P*	*S*	
	Parental prop. you got?	*No./%*	*No./%*	*No./%*	*No./%*	*No./%*	*No./%*	*No./%*
	Total	788	788	788	788	788	788	
		100.00	100.00	100.00	100.00	100.00	100.00	100.00

The Table 11 reveals the urban-rural differences in giving due share to daughters [especially after their marriage] from their parental property. While comparatively lesser share was given to daughters in rural areas, there prevailed the opposite situation in the urban areas. However, it was also revealed that more and more people become aware about paying due share to daughters in the total property.

3.12. Marital Ralations after Marriage

Another crucial problem faced by women after marriage is related with the role of girls in in-laws family. Normally, a girl in Kashmir gets married and goes to the husband's home to settle there. There she has to adjust and compromise in many ways. If she succeeds in adjusting there, it is followed by harmony in relations with members in in-laws family. If she fails, it is followed by conflict in relations with members of in-laws family. In some cases, the members in in-laws family start teasing consciously and purposefully the girl just after marriage. They create a lot of problems for the girl. In some cases, the extreme teasing/torture compels the newly-married girl to commit suicide or the in-laws kill her. In this background, we made a relevant inquiry. We characterized the relations in family good and bad. While the former refers to the harmonious type of relations between the girl and other members of in-laws family, the latter means conflict type of relations. The response we received has been noted in the Table 12.

Table 12
MARITAL RELATIONS IN IN-LAWS FAMILY

S.No	Theme/Question Girls relations with		A No./%	B No./%	B No./%	K No./%	P No./%	S No./%	Total No./%
1.	Husband	-Good	500 62.50	452 56.50	500 62.50	475 79.12	600 89.95	500 98.03	3027 88.19
		-Bad	33 11.12	110 13.75	60 9.50	125 20.83	67 10.04	10 1.96	405 11.80
2.	Father-in-Law	-Good	321 40.12	495 61.87	500 62.50	433 72.16	427 44.01	390 76.47	2566 74.75
		-Bad	212 76.50	67 8.37	60 7.50	167 27.83	240 35.98	120 23.52	866 25.23
3.	Mother-in-Law	-Good	346 43.47	366 45.75	490 61325	490 65.00	520 77.96	221 43.33	2332 67.94
		-Bad	188 23.50	196 24.50	70 8.75	210 35.00	147 22.03	289 56.11	1100 32.05
4.	Sister-in-Law	-Good	256 44.37	464 50.50	40 50.00	280 46.66	501 25.11	220 43.13	2221 64.71
		-Bad	177 22.72	98 12.25	110 13.75	320 53.34	166 24.88	290 50.86	1161 33.82

The table 12 conveys that majority of girls had established harmonious type of relations with members of in-laws family and it was not possible for minority of girls. In the case of husband, the girls had established good relations in the 88.19 per cent cases.

However, 74.76 per cent girls only had harmonious type of relations with their fathers-in-law. The situation was not the same vis-a-vis mothers-in-law and sisters-in-law. Only 67.94 per cent 64.71 per cent girls had established harmonious type of relations.

3.13. Practice of Beating of Wives

If the relations between the girls and in-laws family members remain bad for a longer time, it may lead to extreme deterioration and degeneration in the relations between the girls and their husbands. This situation crudely reflects in the practice of beating wives. Our investigation in this regard gave us the following information:

Table13
PRACTICE OF WIFE-BEATING

S.No	Theme/Question	Respondents [district-wise]						Total
	Do your husband	A	B	B	K	P	S	
	beat you?	No./%	No./%	No./%	No./%	No./%	No./%	No./%
1.	Yes	59	128	100	120	79	98	584
		7.33	16.00	12.50	15.00	9.87	12.25	12.16
2.	No	474	424	460	480	588	412	2848
		59.33	66.75	57.50	60.00	73.50	5.80	57.33
3.	N.A/N.R.	267	298	240	200	133	290	1385
		33.33	29.25	30.00	25.00	16.62	36.25	28.50
	Total	800	800	800	800	800	800	4800
		100.00	100.00	100.00	100.00	100.00	100.00	100.00

The Table 13 shows that while 584/4800 [12.16 per cent] women respondents were beaten by their husbands [regularly or occasionally], 2848/4800 [59.33 per cent] respondents had no such experience. The practice of wife-beating is not reported fully by the respondents. It is hidden because of social reaction against the concerned husbands. However, we feel that the data in the table is indicative and tells about the trend of this practice.It is important to note here that wife-beating is not reported fully by the respondents. It is hidden because of social reaction against the concerned husbands. However, we feel that the data in the table is indicative and tells about the trend of this practice.

3.14. Places of Work of Working Women

It has been observed that women faced one set of problems in the traditional situation. In the changing situation, especially when women started working outside their homes, new problems for women were added. When women go outside their homes and stay there for most of the day time, it creates several crucial problems which include emergence of dual role, conflict in the home, lesser time for child care, and harassment. Women face many problems mainly because of working in outside home places like offices. In this connection, we made an inquiry about the places of work of women respondents. The response we got has been entered in the following Table 14.

Table 14
PLACE OF WORK OF WORKING WOMEN

S.No	*Theme/Question*	*Respondents [district-wise]*						*Total*
	Place of work	*A*	*B*	*B*	*K*	*P*	*S*	
		No./%	*No./%*	*No./%*	*No./%*	*No./%*	*No./%*	*No./%*
1.	Govt.Office	23 38.98	74 47.70	100 80.00	80 60.00	40 30.00	202 67.3	519 65.77

(Contd.)

(Contd. Table 14)

S.No	Theme/Question	Respondents [district-wise]						Total
	Place of work	A	B	B	K	P	S	
		No./%	No./%	No./%	No./%	No./%	No./%	No./%
2.	Non-Govt.Office	36	81	25	20	10	98	230
		61.01	52.20	20.00	20.00	20.00	32.66	34.22
3.	Nearby place	42	102	75	70	30	60	379
		71.00	65.80	60.00	70.00	60.00	20.00	48.03
4.	Far off place	17	53	50	30	20	240	410
		29.00	34.19	40.00	30.00	20.00	80.00	31.96
	Total	59	155	125	100	50	300	789
		100.00	100.00	100.00	100.00	100.00	100.00	16.43

The Table 14 reveals that while 65.77 per cent respondents work in the government offices, 34.22 per cent respondents work in non-governmental offices. It was conveyed that more problems for women were created in non-governmental offices than in the governmental offices. Moreover, if complainer action against defaulters was taken in the governmental offices than in the non-governmental offices. Again, more problems were created for women in the offices located at far off places than in the nearby offices.

3.15. Emergence of Dual Role of Women

One of the crucial implications of the women's work outside their homes led to the emergence of dual role for them. It means the working women have to work at two places,office and home. This has given the working women tough time and created many problems for themselves, their family members, especially children. In this thematic context, we inquired among the women respondents. The response we got has been noted in the following Table 15:

Table 15
DUAL ROLE OF WOMEN

S.No	*Theme/Question*	*Respondents [district-wise]*						*Total*
	Have you developed	*A*	*B*	*B*	*K*	*P*	*S*	
	Dual role?	*No./%*	*No./%*	*No./%*	*No./%*	*No./%*	*No./%*	*No./%*
1.	Yes	27	140	75	41	30	150	463
		45.76	90.32	60.00	41.00	60.00	50.00	58.68
2.	No.	32	5	50	59	20	150	316
		54.23	3.22	40.00	59.00	40.00	30.00	40.50

The Table 15 shows that majority of working women 463, [58.68 per cent] had developed dual role, while minority of respondents 316, [40.50 per cent] had not developed this role. This response was shown more in the urban areas than in the rural areas.

3.16. Problems of Child Care

Another crucial implication of the adoption of the Working role by women was felt in the rise of problems related to child care at home. In a situation in which women remain outside their homes, the child care has emerged as a big question. Though this problem has been taken care of in joint family, it still exists as the crucial problem in the nuclear family. Consequently, the children especially the infants, suffer absolutely. They are taken care of by others than their parents. but it has different effects on child's personality, particularly related to socialization. We made an inquiry in this background and the results have been noted in the following Table 16:

Table 16
CHILD CARE AT HOME

S.No	Theme/Question	Respondents [district-wise]						Total
	Who takes care of the	A	B	B	K	P	S	
	Child during the day?	No./%	No./%	No./%	No./%	No./%	No./%	No./%
1.	Husband's family	41 69.49	34 21.93	99 79.20	65 65.00	25 5.00	103 43.33	394 49.93
2.	Parent's family	11 18.64	86 55.43	20 16.00	25 25.00	17 30.00	120 40.00	279 35.36
3.	Servant/Maid	5 8.47	20 12.20	6 4.80	10 10.00	3 600	35 11.66	79 10.01
4.	Others	2 3.38	5 3.22	00 00.00	00 00.00	0 00.00	5 1.66	12 1.52
5.	N.A/N.R.	00 00	10 6.45	00 00.00	00 00.00	5 00.00	10 3.33	25 3.16
	Total	59 100.00	155 100.00	125 100.00	100 100.00	50 100.00	300 100.00	789 16.43

The Table 16 shows all those families whose women go outside their homes regularly suffer in terms of non-care of children during the day time. In that situation, the respondents husband's family and the respondents parent's family came to the rescue of the working women. While 49.93 per cent respondents children are taken care of by their husband's family, 35.36 per cent respondents children remain at their parent's family. Moreover, children of 10.01 per cent respondents are taken care of by servants/ maids.

3.17. Impact on the Socialization of Children

As mentioned in the previous section, the adoption of the working career by women had direct negative effect on the personality development of children, especially the infants. They also suffer in socialization. We made an inquiry in this matter and got the response included in the Table 17:

Table 17
IMPACT OF WORKING CAREER ON THE SOCIALIZATION OF CHILDREN

S.No	*Theme/Question*	*Respondents [district-wise]*						*Total*
	Nature of Impact	*A*	*B*	*B*	*K*	*P*	*S*	
		No./%	*No./%*	*No./%*	*No./%*	*No./%*	*No./%*	*No./%*
1.	Positive	20	69	80	76	40	210	495
		33.89	44.1	64.00	76.00	80.00	70.00	62.75
2.	Negative	30	76	35	24	10	70	245
		50.84	49.03	28.00	24.00	20.00	23.33	31.05
3.	N.A/N.R.	9	10	10	00	00	20	49
		15.25	6.45	8.00	00	00	6.66	6.21
	Total	59	155	125	100	50	300	789
		100.00	100.00	100.00	100.00	100.00	100.00	100.00

The Table 17 reveals that a significant proportion of women respondents, 245/789 [31.05 per cent] experienced negative implications 011 their children. They gave the examples of deviance, lesser social control, abuse of authority in the family and so on. Other children, i.e. 62.73 per cent, reported the negative impact on children by keeping children in the custody/control of their own parents or with those members of in-laws family who usually stay at home.

3.18. Impact of Working Career on the Family

In continuation of the preceding sections, this section deals with the nature of impact of the working career on family. Our investigation in this regard gave the following responses:

Table 18
IMPACT OF THE WORKING CAREER ON FAMILY

S.No	Theme/Question Nature of Impact	Respondents [district-wise] A No./%	B No./%	B No./%	K No./%	P No./%	S No./%	Total No./%
1.	Increase in deviance among children	12 40.00	30 30.00	12 12.00	8 33.33	10 100.00	41 58.59	113 46.12
2.	Decreasing social control within families	14 46.16	20 26.31	12 34.28	10 41.66	00 00	16 23.85	72 29.38
3.	Various social issues	4 13.33	26 34.21	11 31.42	6 25.00	00 00	13 18.59	60 24.48
	Total	30 100.00	76 100.00	35 100.00	24 100.00	10 100.00	70 100.00	245 100.00

The Table 18 reveals three aspects of impact of the emergence of working role of women with the focus on children. Significant number of children, 46.12 per cent, have developed various trends of deviance which resulted in the partial change in the traditional ethos. Second, this impact also reflected in the failure in various degree of social control within the context of family. This was revealed by 29.38 per cent respondents. Finally, 24.48 per cent respondents reported emergence of various social problems due to the adoption of working role by women. These social problems include improper socialization, conflict situation, marital disharmony and so on.

3.19. Impact on Domestic Relations

In continuation of the theme of previous sections, we inquired in this section about the nature of impact of the adoption of working role by women on the domestic relations. The respondents' response reflect in the following Table 19:

Table 19
IMPACT ON DOMESTIC RELATIONS

S.No	Theme/Question		Respondents [district-wise]						Total
	Nature of Impact		A	B	B	K	. P	S	
			No./%	No./%	No./%	No./%	No./%	No./%	No./%
1.	Relations with	Good	50	102	107	75	41	190	558
	Husband		34.74	65.80	80.00	75.00	82.00	63.33	70.72
		Bad	9	53	25	25	9	110	231
			15.35	34.19	20.00	25.00	18.00	36.66	29.20
2.	Relations with	Good	40	32	95	80	30	130	407
	in-laws		67.79	20.64	76.00	8.00	60.00	93.00	52.53
		Bad	19	123	30	20	20	170	352
			32.20	79.35	24.00	28.00	40.00	56.66	43.41
3.	Relations with	Good	40	78	110	60	35	180	512
	near-relatives		83.05	50.32	68.00	60.00	70.00	60.00	64.89
		Bad	10	77	15	40	15	120	277
			16.94	49.69	12.00	60.00	30.00	40.00	35.10

4

Economic Problems

4.1. Pattern of Traditional Occupation

Generally, the inhabitants of the land-locked valley of Kashmir were carrying out the economic activities in the past, which were mainly consumption-oriented rather than market-oriented. Simultaneously, they were engaged in other economic activities which could give them *some* amount of *money.* The adoption of the handicraft works by a significant portion of the Kashmiri people in the medieval times may be cited in this regard. Our inquiry revealed the traditional pattern of economic activities/occupations which has been shown in the Table 1.

The Table 1 reveals that the *most* significant group among respondents in rural as well as urban areas was engaged in agriculture. This group dominates other groups [from 37.50 per cent to 80.00 per cent] except in Sri nagar district where only 5.00 per cent people were engaged in agriculture. Other significant group of respondents was engaged in different sectors of handicrafts. Again the number of handicraft men and women are numerically least in Sri nagar district [49, i.e. 6.12 per cent] than in other districts in the Kashmir valley. Another significant group was engaged in economic activities related to small business which included the selling of handicraft items. This group composed of 273, i.e. 7.77 per cent.

Table 1
PATTERN OF TRADITIONAL ECONOMIC ACTIVITIES/ OCCUPATIONS

S.No	*Theme/Question*	*Respondents [district-wise]*						*Total*
	Traditional Occupation	*A*	*B*	*B*	*K*	*P*	*S*	
		No./%	*No./%*	*No./%*	*No./%*	*No./%*	*No./%*	*No./%*
1.	Agriculture	300	200	380	400	350	120	1730
		37.50	80.00	45.00	50.00	43.75	15.00	36.00
2.	Handicraft	233	64	202	175	144	49	867
		29.12	8.00	25.75	21.87	18.00	6.12	18.06
3.	Small Business	107	16	59	60	71	60	373
		13.37	2.00	6.12	7.5	8.87	7.50	7.77
4.	H.H. Occupations	36	48	49	40	95	101	369
		4.5	6.00	6.12	5.00	11.87	12.62	7.68
5.	Other Eco. Activities	124	32	130	125	130	470	1911
		15.50	4.00	1625	15.62	16.25	58.75	21.06
	Total	800	800	800	800	800	800	4800
		100.00	100.00	100.00	100.00	100.00	100.00	100.00

4.2. Change in Traditional Occupations

The centuries old traditional occupational structure in Kashmir could not remain intact in modern times. Various processes of modernisation, especially development and change. in the recent past have changed partly or fully the traditional occupations and created new occupations. Our inquiry about change in traditional occupations got the response recorded in the following table:

Table 2
CHANGE IN THE TRADITIONAL OCCUPATIONS

S.No	*Theme/Question*	*Respondents [district-wise]*						*Total*
	Have your family	*A*	*B*	*B*	*K*	*P*	*S*	
	Occupation experienced change?	*No./%*	*No./%*	*No./%*	*No./%*	*No./%*	*No./%*	*No./%*
1.	Yes	432	550	221	269	310	475	2250
		54.00	68.75	27.62	33.62	38.75	59.37	47.00
2.	No	368	250	579	541	490	325	2558
		46.00	31.25	72.37	67.62	61.35	40.62	53.18
	Total	800	800	800	800	800	800	800
		100.00	100.00	100.00	100.00	100.00	100.00	100.00

The Table 2 shows clearly that 47.00 per cent respondents and their families have undergone the occupational mobility/change in the recent past, especially after 1947. On the Other hand, 53.18 per cent respondents and their families have continued with their traditional economic activities with certain revisions and improvements.

4.3. Pattern of Occupational Change / Mobility

It became clear from the previous section that a significant number of respondents and their families have undergone change in their traditional economic activities. It follows that these families

Table 3
PATTERN OF OCCUPATIONAL CHANGE

S.No	Theme/Question	Respondents [district-wise]						Total
	New occupations/eco activities adopted	A	B	B	K	P	S	
		No./%	No./%	No./%	No./%	No./%	No./%	No./%
1.	Govt. Service	210	300	180	117	120	330	1257
		48.61	54.50	61.44	43.49	30.90	69.49	55.59
2.	Handicrafts	15	50	15	35	20	30	165
		3.47	9.09	6.78	13.01	6345	6.31	7.31
3.	Small industries	23	41	-	65	10	20	159
		5.32	7.45	-	24.16	3.22	4.21	7.04
4.	Non-Govt Service	23	41	-	65	10	20	159
		5.32	7.45	-	24.16	3.22	4.21	7.04
5.	Horticulture	19	18	-	-	-	-	37
		4.39	3.27	-	-	-	-	1.63
6	No Occupational Change	368	250	579	541	490	325	2553
		46.00	31.35	72.37	67.62	61.25	40.62	53.18
	Total	800	800	800	800	800	800	4800
		100.00	100.00	100.00	100.00	100.00	100.00	100.00

have adopted partly or wholly new occupations/economic activities. In fact, this was must in the new situation created by the processes of development and change. Our investigation in this field got the response noted in the following Table 3:

The Table 3 reveals that 47.02 per cent respondents and their families had experienced partial or complete change in their economic activities/occupations This kind of change was felt more in the urban areas than in the rural areas. Thus this change was reported by 59.37 per cent respondents in Srinagar district in comparison to 27.62 per cent in Budgam district and 54.00 per cent in Anantnag district. A significant number of respondents, 2553, i.e. 53.18 per cent, had not experienced the radical change in the economic field. Finally, the table shows that economic activities in some new sectors had been initiated as follows:

(a) Government service 55.69 per cent
(b) Non-government service 7.04 per cent
(c) Horticulture 1.63 per cent

4.4. Pattern of Women's Work on Land

Generaly women in rural Kashmir work with men on their land. This work of women stands as the potential contribution to the rural economy dominated by agriculture. They are lot paid wages for this because they work on their own lands. However, in some exceptional cases, some women work on other lands, for which they are paid. Our inquiry on this theme of the response has been entered in the Table 4. The Table 4 portrays that 2625/4800 [54.68 per cent] respondents worked on the agricultural land. Among them, 89.33 per cent worked on their own lands and 10.66 per cent worked on others lands. Those who didn't work on the agricultural land numbered 2175 [45.31 per cent].

Table 4
WOMEN'S WORK ON AGRICULTURAL LAND

S.No	Theme/Question	Respondents [district-wise]						Total
	Do you work on land?	A	B	B	K	P	S	
		No./%	No./%	No./%	No./%	No./%	No./%	No./%
1.	Yes	572	563	400	500	490	100	2625
		71.50	70.30	50.00	62.50	61.25	12.50	54.65
	-on self land	566	544	380	320	450	85	2345
		98.85	96.62	25.00	64.00	91.83	85.00	89.33
	-on others land	6	19	20	180	40	15	280
		1.05	3.37	5.00	36.00	8.16	15.00	10.66
	Total	800	800	800	800	800	800	4800
		100.00	100.00	100.00	100.00	100.00	100.00	100.00

In fact, the share of women working on agricultural land is reducing further because women, after education, opt for other careers. While the response in all districts is similar, the response of the Sri nagar district is dissimilar. It shows while 100 [12.50 per cent] respondents work on the agricultural land, 700 [82.50 per cent] are busy in other sectors.This is because this distinct is mostly urban in which most of the people work in non- agricultural sectors.

4.5. Payment of Wages to Women Workers

As is clear from the previous table, rural women in Kashmir work on the agricultural land. While many among them work on their own lands, others, very less in number, work on others lands.

The work on others lands by women is because of compulsive and economic reasons. While the former group of women don't get wages for the work, the later group of women get wages, in terms of cash or commodity, regularly. Their proportion and conditions of wages has been noted in the Table 5.

Table 5
WOMEN'S WORK ON AGRICULTURAL LAND

S.No	Theme/Question	Respondents [district-wise]						Total
	Do you get wages for?	A	B	B	K	P	S	
	Your work on other land?	No./%	No./%	No./%	No./%	No./%	No./%	No./%
1.	Yes [working on others land]	6 1.04	19 3.37	20 5.00	180 36.00	40 8.16	15 1.15	280 10.66
2.	No [working on their own land]	566 98.95	544 96.67	380 95.00	320 64.00	450 91.83	85 65.00	2345 89.33
	Total	572 100.00	563 100.00	400 100.00	800 100.00	500 100.00	490 100.00	2625 100.00

The Table 5 shows that the number of respondents who worked on others agricultural land is 280 (10.66 per cent]. They reported that they get the wages regularly. In response to our particular question regarding the amount of wages, they gave the following answers:

(a) Wages are sufficient 20 (07.14 per cent] respondents;
(b) Wages are not sufficient 260 (72.85 per cent] respondents.

Those respondents who said no [2345, 89.33 per cent] were

working on their own land. So, there was no need to pay the wages.

4.6. Women Workers in the Handicraft Sector

Another economic sector in which women work in large number, including the girl children, is the handicraft sector. In all fields of the I1andicraft sector, women work in rural as well as in urban areas, though in different numbers. The factual situation in this regard reflects in the Table 6.

Table 6
WOMEN'S WORK IN THE HANDICRAFT SECTOR

S.No	Theme/Question	Respondents [district-wise]						Total
	In which hadicraft Sector / field you work?	A	B	B	K	P	S	
		No./%	No./%	No./%	No./%	No./%	No./%	No./%
1.	Yes	233 100.00	302 100.00	430 100.00	100 100.00	200 100.00	210 100.00	1455 100.00
2.	Field: Shawibati	50 21.45	63 2086	310 73.80	15 15.00	80 40.00	30 14.28	548 37.40
3.	Kaleenbati	110 47.23	54 17.88	50 11.90	20 20.00	20 10.00	20 9.52	274 18.70
4.	Shahtos-phum weaving	36 15.45	70 23.12	10 2.38	5 6.00	30 15.00	20 23.80	274 13.72
5.	Paper machine	15 6.43	17 5.62	- -	- -	5 3.50	40 19.04	77 5.25

(Contd.)

(Contd. Table 6)

S.No	*Theme/Question*	*Respondents [district-wise]*						*Total*
	In which hadicraft Sector / field you work?	*A*	*B*	*B*	*K*	*P*	*S*	
		No./%	*No./%*	*No./%*	*No./%*	*No./%*	*No./%*	*No./%*
6.	Wood carving	15	23	-	-	-	-	3
		6.43	7.61	-	-	-	-	2.54
7.	Crewel work	3	30	40	50	55	50	228
		1.28	9.92	2.52	50.00	27.50	23.80	15.56

The Table 6 conveys that a significant number of women workers are engaged in different fields of the handicraft sector. Their number is 1465/4800 which is 30.52 per cent of the total respondents. Many girl children are also working in this sector, especially in the fields of shawlbati, paper machine and crewel work. It is also clear that most of the women workers work in the field of shawlbati [37.40 per cent] and *Kaleenbati* [18.30]

4.7. Wages to Women Workers in Handicraft Secotor

It is generally upheld by the experts and others concerned that women working in different fields of handicrafts, with the sole purpose of earning money, are not paid due wages for their hard labour. They generally get lesser wages than they deserve. It happens because of two major reasons. First, the standard rates for working on different handicraft items have not been fixed by the government. Second, in the absence of standard rates, the big and small handicraft businessmen manipulate the concerned market and decide the wages of all handicraft items on their own. Thus the handicraft workers have no say in the fixation of their wages. Consequently, they suffer absolutely and get trapped in the manipulative system in which they are not able to come out throughout their life-span. Our investigation in this matter gave us the information included in the Table 7.

Table 7
PAYMENT OF WAGES TO WOMEN WORKERS

S..No	Theme/Question	Respondents [district-wise]						Total
	In which hadicraft	A	B	B	K	P	S	
	Sector / field you	No./%	No./%	No./%	No./%	No./%	No./%	No./%
1.	Yes	33	78	20	25	30	40	226
		14.66	25.02	4.76	25.00	15.00	19.04	15.42
2.	No	200	234	400	75	170	170	1239
		85.83	74.17	95.23	75.00	85.00	80.95	84.57

The Table 7 reveals that 226 [15.2 per cent] respondents get due wages for their work on handicraft items. When we inquired whether these wages fulfill your basic needs of life, their response was as follows:

(a) Yes 116 [51.32 per cent] respondents
(b) No 110 [48.67 per cent] respondents

On the other hand, majority of respondents working in the handicraft sector [1239, 84.57 per cent] said that they were not getting due wages for the handicraft work they perform.

4.8. Exploitation of Women Workers

As became clear from the preceding table, women workers in the handicraft sector were not getting due wages for their work.

Thus they felt exploited extremely at the hands of middlemen and wholesalers in the handicraft business. These workers argue that taking into consideration the labour input and the wages output, the large and small businessmen in handicrafts get the maximum monetary benefits, while they share the least monetary benefits. Our research in this problem gave us the information which has been noted in the Table 8.

Table 8

EXPLOITATION OF WOMEN WORKERS

S..No	*Theme/Question*	*Respondents [district-wise]*						*Total*
	Do you feel you get exploited ?	*A*	*B*	*B*	*K*	*P*	*S*	
		No./%	*No./%*	*No./%*	*No./%*	*No./%*	*No./%*	*No./%*
1.	Yes	200 85.03	224 70.17	400 75.23	75 75.00	170 85.00	170 80.95	1237 84.57
2.	No	33 14.16	78 25.82	20 4.75	25 25.00	30 15.00	40 19.04	226 15.42
	Total	233 100.00	292 100.00	420 100.00	100 100.00	200 100.00	210 100.00	465 100.00

The Table 8 reveals clearly that huge majority of respondents were getting exploited at *the* hands of small and big handicraft businessmen. 1239 respondents showed this response. On the other hand, 226 [15.42 per cent] respondents felt that they were not getting exploited. In fact. they too get exploited more or less. But, they are not conscious about it.

4.9. Women Work Outside their Homes

When women get modern education, they feel compelled to work outside their homes earning money. In this situation, they have to work in the governmental as well as non-governmental offices, which are located in the near-by or far off areas. The problems of working women are also determined by the offices or places of their work. In this regard, our inquiry gave the information in Table 9.

Table 9
PLACES OF WORK OF THE WORKING WOMEN

S..No	*Theme/Question*	*Respondents [district-wise]*						*Total*
	Are you working in	*A*	*B*	*B*	*K*	*P*	*S*	
		No./%	*No./%*	*No./%*	*No./%*	*No./%*	*No./%*	*No./%*
1.	Government Office	23	84	100	80	40	202	529
		38.98	54.19	80.00	80.00	80.00	67.33	67.04
2.	Non-Govt. Office	36	17	25	20	10	98	260
		61.01	45.80	20.00	20.00	20.00	32.00	32.92
3.	Location of Office							
	-in your area	42	102	75	70	30	60	379
		71.00	65.80	40.00	30.00	40.00	80.00	48.03
	-in other area	17	53	5	30	20	240	410
		29.00	34.19	40.00	30.00	40.00	80.00	51.96
	Total	59	155	125	100	50	300	789
		100.00	100.00	100.00	100.00	100.00	100.00	100.00

The Table 9 reveals that majority of the working women respondents [*529/789,* 67.04 per cent] were working in the government offices where they faced lesser problems in comparison to those who were working in non-government offices whose number was 260 [32.95 per cent]. On the other hand, the location of the office too contributed to the problems of working women. In our survey, while *379n89* [48.03 per cent] respondents worked in near-by area office, *410/789* [51.96 per cent] respondents had to go far off area office.

4.10. Amount of Salary of Working Women

The preceding sections make it clear that a certain number of women work in the offices and other places for earning money. Like their counterparts, the women get different levels of salary which depends upon the formal positions they occupy in their respective offices. Our inquiry in this regard gave us the information noted in theTable 10.

Table 10

AMOUNT OF SALARY TO THE WORKING WOMEN

S.No	*Theme/Question*	*Respondents [district-wise]*						*Total*
	Regular Salary of the	*A*	*B*	*B*	*K*	*P*	*S*	
	Working woman[p.m.]	*No./%*	*No./%*	*No./%*	*No./%*	*No./%*	*No./%*	*No./%*
1.	Upto Rs. 5000/-	40	98	60	71	20	110	394
		67.79	8312	48.00	71.00	40.00	36.66	47.93
2.	Between 5001-10,000/-	15	53	60	26	29	175	358
		25.42	34.19	48.00	26.00	58.00	58.33	45.37

(Contd.)

(Contd. Table 10)

S..No	Theme/Question	Respondents [district-wise]						Total
	Does regular salary give	A	B	B	K	P	S	
	You eco.Independenc?	No./%	No./%	No./%	No./%	No./%	No./%	No./%
3.	Rs.10001/- & above	4	9	5	3	1	15	37
		6.77	5.80	4.00	3.00	2.00	5.00	4.88
	Total	59	155	125	100	50	300	789
		100.00	100.00	100.00	100.00	100.00	100.00	100.00

The statistical details in the above table reveal that huge salaries. On the other hand, women working on gazetted and other supervisory positions number only 37 which composes 4.65 per cent of total working women.

4.11. Regular Salary and Economic Independence

It has generally been assumed that the regular salary of working women gives them much desired economic independence. They earn themselves and spend themselves according to their own priorities. But, still some women don't get the desirable economic independence. Our investigation in this regard gave the information recorded in the following Table 11.

The Table 11 shows that while 572/789 [72.49 per cent] respondents enjoy the economic independence mainly due to getting regular salary and spending themselves, 217/789 [27.50 per cent] respondents gave the opposite response. In actuality, the economic independence of working women depends whether they keep the salary with themselves or hand over to their in-laws. In the latter case, there seems less possibility to develop economic independence.

Table 11
REGULAR SALARY AND ECONOMIC INDEPENDENCE OF WORKING WOMEN

S..No	Theme/Question	Respondents [district-wise]						Total
	Does regular salary give	A	B	B	K	P	S	
	You eco.Independenc?	No./%	No./%	No./%	No./%	No./%	No./%	No./%
1.	Yes	50 84.74	92 54.35	110 88.00	60 60.00	50 100.00	210 70.00	572 72.49
2.	No	9 15.05	63 40.64	15 12.00	40 40.00	- -	90 30.00	217 27.50
	Total	59 100.00	155 100.00	125 100.00	100 100.00	50 100.00	300 100.00	789 100.00

4.12. Pattern of Spending by Working Women

It became evident in the previous section that the economic independence of the working women start with earning themselves and spending themselves as well. They spend according to their priorities, choices and requirements. We inquired about the established pattern of behaviour of working women in this regard. The response we received has been entered in the Table 12.

Table 12
PATTERNS OF SPENDING BY WORKING WOMEN

S.No	Theme/Question	Respondents [district-wise]						Total
	Do you spend your	A	B	B	K	P	S	
	Income yourself?	No./%	No./%	No./%	No./%	No./%	No./%	No./%
1.	Yes	19 32.20	125 86.04	49 32.00	33 33.00	30 60.00	205 68.33	452 57.23

(Contd.)

(Contd. Table 12)

S.No	Theme/Question	Respondents [district-wise]						Total
	Do you spend your	A	B	B	K	P	S	
	Income yourself?	No./%	No./%	No./%	No./%	No./%	No./%	No./%
2.	No	45	30	85	67	20	95	342
		76.27	14.27	68.00	67.00	40.00	31.66	43.34

The Table 12 reveals that majority of the working women respondents [452: 52.28 per cent] spend their money themselves and bought the required items from the market. On the 'other hand, minority of respondents didn't spend their money solely but in the company of their husbands and/or other family members. When we inquired about the purpose of spending, the respondents gave the following answer:

(a) self needs only — 57.14 per cent respondents;

(b) family needs — 42.86 per cent respondents.

This response makes it clear that working women spend their hard-earned money for self as well as for family needs. But, the difference in this pattern of spending is that they take the initiative and spend independently without any dependence or direction of others.

4.13. Economic Activities Performed by Women

In order 10 get an overall view of the economic activities performed by women in rural and urban areas in the Kashmir valley at present, we asked the relevant questions. In response, they referred to several economic activities, among which we took three top-rated activities in rural as well as in urban areas. The details follow in the Table 13.

Table 13
ECONOMIC ACTIVITIES PERFORMED BY WOMEN [AREA-WISE]

S.No	*Theme/Question*	*Respondents [district-wise]*						*Total*
	Nature of Economic	*A*	*B*	*B*	*K*	*P*	*S*	
	Activity [area-wise]	*No./%*	*No./%*	*No./%*	*No./%*	*No./%*	*No./%*	*No./%*
Rural Area:								
1.	Agriculture	240	210	200	500	375	-	1625
		30.00	26.25	25.00	62.50	46.87	12.50	33.55
2.	Handicrafts	200	172	360	75	160	50	1017
		25.00	21.50	45.00	9.37	20.00	6.75	21.68
3.	Harti-Floriculture	-	50	-	30	-	-	80
		-	6.25	-	3.75	-	-	9.66
Urban Area:								
1.	Govt. Service	23	74	100	80	40	202	519
		2.87	9.25	12.50	10.00	5.00	25.25	10.89
2.	Non-Govt. Service	36	81	25	20	10	98	270
		4.50	10.12	3.12	2.50	1.25	12.25	5.
3.	Handicrafts	33	130	60	25	40	160	448
		4.12	16.25	7.50	3.12	5.00	20.00	9.33

(Contd.)

(Contd. Table 13)

S.No	Theme/Question	Respondents [district-wise]						Total
	Nature of Economic	A	B	B	K	P	S	
	Activity [area-wise]	No./%	No./%	No./%	No./%	No./%	No./%	No./%
4.	N.A/N.R.	268	832	55	70	175	190	841
		22.50	10.37	6.87	8.75	21.53	23.75	17.90
	Total	800	800	800	800	800	800	4800
		100.00	100.00	100.00	100.00	100.00	100.00	100.00

It is clear from the table 13 that while economic activities related to agriculture, handicrafts and horticulture-floriculture dominate in the rural areas, economic activities related to govt. non-govt. service and handicrafts dominate the urban areas. It also revealed that while consumption-oriented as well as market-oriented economic sectors prevail in the rural areas, the market-oriented economic sectors only prevail in the urban areas. We also inquired about the payment of wages to the women if they work in any or all sectors of economy. They gave the following response:

(a) Yes 52.39 per cent respondents
(b) No 32.27 per cent respondents
(c) N.A./N.R. 15.33 per cent respondents

4.14. Educated Women and Government Jobs

It has been observed that women in Kashmir, after getting education, want to get the govt. jobs at any cost. .Many experts feel that women here start trying to get govt. jobs just after passing out the Matriculation examination. But, on the other hand, there is absolute scarcity of govt. jobs in the state. Thus this problem engulfs them at very early age. In this context, our investigation gave the information included in the Table 14.

Table 14

EDUCATED WOMEN AND GOVERNMENT JOBS

S.No	Theme/Question	Respondents [district-wise]						Total
	Should girls get govt.	A	B	B	K	P	S	
	Jobs just after Matric	No./%	No./%	No./%	No./%	No./%	No./%	No./%
1.	Yes	610	640	460	514	610	700	3534
		76.25	80.00	57.50	64.25	76.25	87.50	73.62
2.	No	130	110	215	187	130	100	872
		16.25	12.5	20.87	23.37	16.25	12.50	18.16
3.	N.A/N.R	60	50	125	99	60	-	394
		7.50	6.75	15.62	12.37	7.50	-	8.20
	Total	800	800	800	800	800	800	4800
		100.00	100.00	100.00	100.00	100.00	100.00	100.00

4.15 Women Benefited by Govt. Programmes

The government at the state as wet as central level has initiated and implemented several programmes and schemes in order to solve crucial problems of women and benefit them in many ways. Some of these programmes have been successful and others have proved failure. In order to assess the benefits to women through these schemes/programmes in the Kashmir valley, we made a relevant inquiry. The response we received has been recorded in the table 15.

Table 15
WOMEN BENEFITED BY GOVERNMENT PROGRAMMES

S..No	Theme/Question	Respondents [district-wise]						Total
	Have you been benefited	A	B	B	K	P	S	
	By any govt. programme?	No./%	No./%	No./%	No./%	No./%	No./%	No./%
1.	Yes	185	236	60	135	50	100	890
		23.12	29.50	9.50	28.12	6.25	12.50	17.63
	-programme							
	-IRDP	10	123	00	20	10	10	173
		5.40	52.11	16.66	13.33	40.00	10.00	54.23
	-TRYSEM	65	45	40	30	20	10	210
		35.13	19.06	16.66	13.33	40.00	10.00	54.23
	-DWCRA	80	32	10	95	10	10	233
		43.24	13.55	16.66	42.22	20.00	10.00	23.68
	-PRY/JRY	-	26	-	-	-	50	76
		-	19.09	-	-	-	50.00	6.89
	-OLD AGE...	30	10	10	80	10	20	160
		6.23	4.23	6.66	35.55	20.00	20.00	18.69
2.	No	615	330	-	-	-	-	234
		76.81	41.25	92.50	7.87	93.75	87.50	77.29
3.	N.A/N.R	-	234	-	-	-	-	234
		-	29.25	-	-	-	-	2.00
	Total	800	800	800	800	800	800	4800
		100.00	100.00	100.00	100.00	100.00	100.00	100.00

5

Educational Problems

5.1. Literacy Among Women

In order to have an overview of the literacy situation prevailing in the Kashmir valley, we asked a direct question to all respondents. Are you a literate person? In response, we got the information which portrays the realistic situation in the valley. This information has been noted in the Table 1:

Table 1
LITERACY AMONG WOMEN

S.No	*Theme/Question*	*Respondents [district-wise]*						*Total*
	Are you a literate	*A*	*B*	*B*	*K*	*P*	*S*	
	Person?	*No./%*	*No./%*	*No./%*	*No./%*	*No./%*	*No./%*	*No./%*
1.	Yes	368	176	150	176	100	450	1420
		46.00	22.00	18.75	22.00	12.50	54.25	29.50
2.	Qualifications: General							
	-Primary	109	57	30	60	32	241	469
		29.61	32.38	20.00	34.09	32.00	44.66	34.43

(Contd.)

(Contd. Table 1)

S.No	Theme/Question	Respondents [district-wise]						Total
	Are you a literate	A	B	B	K	P	S	
	Person?	No./%	No./%	No./%	No./%	No./%	No./%	No./%
	-Middle	90	38	40	35	35	100	338
		24.45	21.59	24.66	19.38	35.00	22.22	23.80
	-Matric	57	34	30	31	10	70	232
		15.48	19.31	20.00	17.61	10.00	15.75	16.33
	-Higher Secondary	60	20	20	19	8	50	177
		16.30	11.36	133	10.69	8.00	11.11	12.46
	-B.A/B.Sc./B.Com.	25	10	25	22	10	10	102
		6.79	10.22	16.66	12.50	10.00	2.22	7.74
	-M.A/M.Sc/M.Com.	10	5	2	1	3	5	26
		2.71	2.86	1.33	0.56	3.00	1.11	1.83
	-Ph.D.	2	1	-	-	-	2	5
		0.50	0.56	-	-	-	0.44	0.35
3.	Qualification[prof./tech]							
	-Medical	5	1	2	5	2	10	25
		1.35	0.56	1.33	1.35	2.00	2.22	1.76
	-Nursing	10	1	1	8	-	2	22
		2.71	0.56	1.33	4.54	-	0.44	1.54
	-Agriculture	-	1	-	2	-	-	3
		-	0.56	-	0.54	-	-	0.21

(Contd.)

(Contd. Table 1)

S.No	Theme/Question	A	B	B	K	P	S	Total
	Are you a literate Person?	*No./%*	*No./%*	*No./%*	*No./%*	*No./%*	*No./%*	*No./%*
4.	No	432	624	650	624	700	350	3380
	Total	800 100.00	800 100.00	800 100.00	800 100.00	800 100.00	800 100.00	4800 100.00

The Table 1 reveals that while 1420/4800 [28.50 per cent] respondents are literate, 3380/4800 [70.41 per cent) respondents are illiterate. It follows that dominant majority of respondents are illiterate while significant minority of respondents are illiterate in rural as well as urban areas. But, this pattern is not followed in district Srinagar where 350/800 [43.75 per cent} are illiterate, while majority of 450/800 [29.70 per cent) respondents are literate. These percentages go in consonance with the census of 1981 and estimates of 1991. It also reveals from the table that heavy majority of respondents pursue general education than those who follow professional and technical education.

5.2. Educated Persons in the Family of Parents

It is generally believed that home environment among other factors, affects all members of the family, especially children, and direct them towards formal education. Thus we may say if parents are educated, there is every possibility of their children getting education. In the same way, other elder member/s in the family effect the attainment or non -attainment of formal education on the part of children in the same family. In the preceding context, we made an inquiry about the educated persons in the family of parents of the respondents. Their response has been arranged in the Table 2.

The Table 2 reveals that significant number of elder members in the families were literate and they had affected their children proportionately. Thus we had following number of educated elders in the families:

(a) Father 31.01 per cent
(b) Mother 15.79 per cent
(c) Brother/s 40.54 per cent
(d) Sister/s 27.93 per cent

Table 2
EDUCATED PERSONS IN THE FAMILY OF PARENTS

S.No	*Theme/Question*	*Respondents [district-wise]*						*Total*
	Educated persons in the Family of parents	*A*	*B*	*B*	*K*	*P*	*S*	
		No./%	*No./%*	*No./%*	*No./%*	*No./%*	*No./%*	*No./%*
1.	Father	190 23.75	160 20.00	200 25.00	103 12.87	190 23.75	450 81.25	1493 31.01
2.	Mother	102 12.75	100 12.50	55 6.87	65 8.12	65 5.62	390 48.75	557 15.79
3.	Brother/s	261 32.62	240 30.00	250 31,50	275 37.37	220 27.50	700 87.50	1946 40.54
4.	Sister/s	180 22.50	140 17.50	101 12.62	155 19.37	165 20.67	600 75.00	1341 27.93

(Contd.)

(Contd. Table 2)

S.No	Theme/Question	Respondents [district-wise]						Total
	Educated persons in the	A	B	B	K	P	S	
	Family of parents	No./%	No./%	No./%	No./%	No./%	No./%	No./%
5.	Others	67 8.37	160 20.00	200 25.00	102 12.50	300 32.50	720 90.00	1519 32.22
	Total	800 100.00	800 100.00	800 100.00	800 100.00	800 100.00	800 100.00	4800 100.00

It was found that more or less same proportion of children in the families were educated. It was primarily because of the impact of elders, especially the parents, in the family.

5.3. Educated Persons in the Family of Husband

Table 3
EDUCATED PERSONS IN THE FAMILY OF HUSBAND

S.No	Theme/Question	Respondents [district-wise]						Total
	Educated persons in the	A	B	B	K	P	S	
	Family of husband	No./%	No./%	No./%	No./%	No./%	No./%	No./%
1.	Father-in-law	165 30.95	175 31.13	200 25.00	121 20.16	145 20.62	400 50.00	1226 25.50
2.	Mother-in-law	100 18.76	95 16.90	69 8.62	80 13.33	60 7.50	211 26.37	615 12.81
3.	Brother/s-in-law	201 37.71	11 28.69	201 25.12	141 23.50	220 23.50	410 51.50	1334 27.70
4.	Sister/s-in-law	195 36.53	124 22.60	101 12.62	65 10.83	185 23.12	320 38.75	980 20.41
5.	Others	300 56.00	201 36.76	200 25.00	189 31.50	301 37.62	500 62.50	1691 35.22

(Contd.)

(Contd. Table 3)

S.No	Theme/Question	Respondents [district-wise]						Total
	Educated persons in the	A	B	B	K	P	S	
	Family of husband	No./%	No./%	No./%	No./%	No./%	No./%	No./%
6.	N.A/N.R.	267	298	240	200	133	290	1368
		-	-	30.00	25.00	6.62	34.25	28.50
	Total	800	800	800	800	800	800	4800
		100.00	100.00	100.00	100.00	100.00	100.00	100.00

More or less the similar response as was reported in the previous section, was shown by the respondents in this section. The details are given in the Table 3.

5.4. Family Education Chart

The Kashmiri society has undergone radical transformation in modern times, especially after 1947. Among other aspects of this situation, this change reflects in the field of education also. In order to know the prevailing situation related to education at the family level, we made a relevant investigation. The response of the respondents reflects in the family education Table 4.

Table 4
FAMILY EDUCATION CHART

S.No	Theme/Question	Respondents [district-wise]						Total
	Educated members in	A	B	B	K	P	S	
	the family	No./%	No./%	No./%	No./%	No./%	No./%	No./%
1.	Total No. of Family members [average]	6.48	6.00	6.80	5.00	6.00	6.40	6.11
2.	No. of Educated [Male]	2.00	1.00	2.20	1.00	2.00	2.00	1.17
	members [Female]	1.58	1.00	1.00	1.00	1.00	2.00	1.26

(Contd.)

(Contd. Table 4)

S.No	Theme/Question	Respondents [district-wise]						Total
	Educated members in	A	B	B	K	P	S	
	The family	No./%	No./%	No./%	No./%	No./%	No./%	No./%
3.	No. of uneducated[Male]	1.15	2.00	1.60	1.00	1.00	1.00	1.90
	members[Female]	1.29	2.00	2.00	2.00	2.00	1.40	1.78
4.	Natural/Level of Edu. General:Primary	-	1.00	1.00	1.00	1.32	0.50	0.80
	Middle	1.00	-	0.09	-	0.25	0.5	0.44
	High	1.50	1.00	1.00	1.00	1.00	1.00	1.09
	H.Secon	1.00	-	0.25	-	0.10	0.50	0.30
	B.A/S.Sc	-	-	0.50	-	0.30	0.50	0.18
	MA/M.Sc	-	-	0.16	-	0.10	0.50	0.12
	M.Phil./Ph.D.	-	-	00	-	00	0.40	0.06
	Prof./Tech	-	-	0.02	-	0.10	0.10	0.03
5.	Place of Education [within J & K State]	3.58	2.00	3.2	2.00	3.00	4.00	-

5.5. Availability of Educational Facilities

It is generally upheld that the educational facilities are available to all the people, especially in the urban areas. These facilities are provided by the governmental as well as non-governmental institutions, organizations and agencies.But, there are some areas, especially in far off villages, where all necessary educational facilities have not been provided. In this context, we made a relevant inquiry and its results have been noted in the Table 5.

Table 5
AVAILABILITY OF EDUCATIONAL FACILITIES

S.No	*Theme/Question*	*Respondents [district-wise]*						*Total*
	Are educational facility	*A*	*B*	*B*	*K*	*P*	*S*	
	Available in your area?	*No./%*	*No./%*	*No./%*	*No./%*	*No./%*	*No./%*	*No./%*
1.	Yes	600 75.00	560 70.00	- 75.00	3000 37.50	550 68.75	720 87.50	3310 60.95
2.	No.	200 25.00	240 28.00	200 25.00	500 62.50	250 31.50	100 12.50	490 30.14

The Table 5 reveals that while 60.95 per cent respondents were getting necessary educational facilities [in terms *of* schools, teachers, equipments and so on], 30.14 per cent respondents were not getting the same facilities. The latter response may apply to the rural and far off areas where neither all schools nor all teachers are available. In these areas, neither school buildings nor required/ trained teachers are available.

5.6. School-going Children in the Family

People in general have started sending their children, both boys and girls, to schools in the previous few decades. In this context, we inquired about the strength *of* school-going children in the family at present. The response we received from the respondents has been entered in the Table 6.

The Table 6 shows that the average rate of school-going children in a family is 2.97 which includes both boys and girls.

However, the rate of male school-going children is 1.71, while the rate of female-children is 1.24. Two aspects of this table are crucial. First, the rate *of* male school-going children is more [1.71 in a family] than the rate *of* female school-going children which is 1.24 in a family. Second, there seems least discrimination against the female children in sending them to the primary school.

Table 6
SCHOOL-GOING CHILDREN IN THE FAMILY

S.No	*Theme/Question*	*Respondents [district-wise]*						*Total*
	No. of school-going child	*A*	*B*	*B*	*K*	*P*	*S*	
	In the family	*No./%*	*No./%*	*No./%*	*No./%*	*No./%*	*No./%*	*No./%*
1.	Total [average]	2.29	3.30	4.20	2.00	2.50	3.50	2.98
2.	Male [average]	1.15	1.70	2.20	1.00	2.00	2.25	1.71
3.	Female [average]	1.14	1.60	2.00	1.00	0.50	1.25	1.24

5.7. Drop Outs from the School

The most crucial problem in the education of children [in terms *of* its devastating implications for children] is their drop-outs from the school at an early stage of formal education. Though the governmental organizations / agencies and non-governmental organizations try to control this phenomenon, they have not succeeded. We made a detailed investigation in this regard. The information we got has been noted in the Table 7.

The Table 7 conveys that 18.00 of the total enrolments in schools have dropped at different stages. Among these drop-outs, girl students are slightly more than boy students. It was also observed that drop-outs at the primary stage are more in comparison with the drop-outs at the middle stage. These are followed by drop-outs at the high [matriculation] stage.

Table 7
NUMBER OF DROP-OUTS FROM THE SCHOOL

S.No	*Theme/Question*	*Respondents [district-wise]*						*Total*
	No. of drop outs from	*A*	*B*	*B*	*K*	*P*	*S*	
	the school	*No./%*	*No./%*	*No./%*	*No./%*	*No./%*	*No./%*	*No./%*
1.	Total	30	20	50	60	60	40	260
2.	Males: Total	16	8	30	32	30	10	126
		52.33	40.00	60.00	53.33	50.00	25.00	21.00
	Primary	12	3	15	15	25	5	75
		75.00	37.50	50.00	46.87	63.33	50.00	12.50
	Middle	2	5	14	12	5	5	43
		12.50	62.50	6.6	37.50	16.66	50.00	12.50
	High	2	-	1	5	-	-	8
		12.50	-	3.33	15.62	-	-	1.33
3.	Females:Total	14	12	20	28	30	30	134
		46.6	60.00	40.00	46.6	50.00	75.00	22.33
	Primary	8	2	8	9	20	15	62
		54.14	16.66	40.00	32.10	66.46	50.00	10.33
	Middle	5	10	8	10	10	10	55
		25.71	83.33	40.00	35.71	33.33	33.33	8.33
	High	1	-	4	7	-	5	19
		7.14	-	20.00	32.14	-	16.66	3.16

5.8. Cost of Education of Children

In the present situation, the cost of education in J&K State is high. There seems every possibility that it will be higher day by day. In the state, education is free in all government schools from primary till university theoretically. But, in the recent past, the government enhanced fee in the government schools virtually negating the concept of free education. As a result of these developments, many students belonging to lower and lower middle classes found it difficult to continue with their education. This situation has increased the cost of education which stands unbearable for significant sections of society. In this context, we inquired from the respondents about the cost of education of their children. Their response has been recorded in the Table 8 which follows:

Table 8
COST OF EDUCATION OF CHILDREN

S.No	Theme/Question	Respondents [district-wise]						Total
	Cost of education of one School- [per month]	A	B	B	K	P	S	
		No./%	No./%	No./%	No./%	No./%	No./%	No./%
1.	Upto Rs.500/-	301 37.62	305 38.12	332 40.35	407 5087	350 43.75	210 26.25	1895 39.67
2.	Rs.501/- Rs.1000/-	195 24.37	192 24.00	200 25.00	140 17.50	290 36.25	290 36.25	1307 27.22
3.	Rs.1001/- & above	37 4.62	65 8.12	238 24.75	53 6.62	27 3.37	10 1.25	430 8.95

(Contd.)

(Contd. Table 8)

S.No	Theme/Question	Respondents [district-wise]						Total
	Cost of education of one School- [per month]	A No./%	B No./%	B No./%	K No./%	P No./%	S No./%	No./%
4.	N.A/N.R.	269 33.37	238 29.75	240 30.00	200 25.00	133 16.62	290 36.25	1368 28.50
	Total	800 100.00	800 100.00	800 100.00	800 100.00	800 100.00	800 100.00	4800 100.00

The above Table 8 conveys that a significant number of respondents, i.e. 1895/4800 [39.67 per cent], spends an amount upto Rs. 500/- per month per child on his / her education. This statement applies to lower and lower-middle classes/groups. Another significant group of 1307/4800 [27.22 per cent] respondents spend an amount between Rs. 501/-. and Rs. 1000/- per month per child on the expenditure related to his/her education.This statement mostly applies to the middle and upper-middle classes. Finally, a small group of 430/4800 [8.95 per cent] respondents revealed that they bear an amount or Rs. 1000/- and above per month per child on education. This statement applies to the upper and upper- middle class families. The children belonging to this category of classes and groups generally study in English-medium, private and missionary schools.

5.9. Children Studying In Govt. / Private Schools

It has generally been observed that children attend different schools in the Urban areas in the valley according to their class background. This reflects of the character of the schools and personalities of children. Our inquiry in this regard gave us the information which has been noted in the Table 9.

Table 9
CHILDREN STUDYING IN GOVT./ PRIVATE SCHOOLS

S.No	*Theme/Question*	*Respondents [district-wise]*						*Total*
	Your child go to the	*A*	*B*	*B*	*K*	*P*	*S*	
		No./%	*No./%*	*No./%*	*No./%*	*No./%*	*No./%*	*No./%*
1.	Government Schools	310	304	325	450	350	190	1929
		38.75	38.00	40.62	56.25	43.75	23.75	40.15
2.	Non-Govt. Schools	223	218	235	150	317	320	1463
		27.87	27.25	29.37	18.75	39.62	40.00	30.47
3.	N.A/N.R.	267	278	240	200	133	290	1408
		33.37	34.75	30.00	25.00	1.62	36.25	28.50
	Total	800	800	800	800	800	800	4800
		100.00	100.00	100.00	100.00	100.00	100.00	100.00

The Table 9 clearly reveals that while 1929/4800 [40.15 per cent] respondents go to the government schools which are located in the access of every village in the valley, 1463/4800 [30.47 per cent] respondents attend the non-government schools, which include private and missionary schools in urban areas. These figures reveal that the study in the school is determined, among other factors, by the economic position of the child's parents. It follows that education has become a commodity and it is your purchasing power which enables you to buy or not to buy this commodity for your child.

It was observed that generally children from lower and lower-middle classes opt for government schools where the fee is very low. On the other hand, children from middle and upper classes join the private, English-medium and missionary schools.

5.10. Career-oriented Education of Children

As education expands in all sections of society, there emerges the need to develop specialization in a particular field. It means that children, after primary education, must opt for that field/ area of education which will be market/development oriented on the one hand and develop professional or technical career. Awareness in this regard is spreading fast. Our inquiry about the awareness among the parents about career-oriented education for their children gave us the information entered in the Table 10.

Table 10
AVARENESS ABOUT CAREER-ORIENTED EDUCATION OF CHILDREN

S.No	*Theme/Question*	*Respondents [district-wise]*						*Total*
	Is the education of your	*A*	*B*	*B*	*K*	*P*	*S*	
	children career-oriented?	*No./%*	*No./%*	*No./%*	*No./%*	*No./%*	*No./%*	*No./%*
1.	Yes	328	195	410	200	380	450	1963
		41.00	24.37	51.25	25.00	47.50	56.25	40.89
	Which type of career?							
	-prof./tech.	170	129	355	125	171	310	1260
		51.82	66.00	86.58	62.50	45.00	68.08	64.18
	-academic	158	66	55	75	209	140	703
		48.17	34.00	13.41	37.50	55.00	31.11	35.81

(Contd.)

(Contd. Table 10)

S.No	Theme/Question	Respondents [district-wise]						Total
	Is the education of your	A	B	B	K	P	S	
	children career-oriented?	No./%	No./%	No./%	No./%	No./%	No./%	No./%
2.	No	205	326	150	300	287	60	1328
		25.62	40.55	18.75	37.50	35.07	7.50	27.66
3.	N.A/N.R.	267	278	240	300	133	290	1368
		33.37	34.75	30.00	37.50	16.62	36.25	28.50
	Total	800	800	800	800	800	800	4800
		100.00	100.00	100.00	100.00	100.00	100.00	100.00

The Table 10 shows that a significant portion of women respondents,1963/4800 [40.89 per cent], are aware about the career-orientation in the education of their children. On the other hand, 1328/4800 [27.66 per cent] respondents were not aware about this. Their children were studying in the general stream.

5.11. Medium of Instruction in the Schools

Different schools in the Kashmir valley have different medium of instruction. While English and Urdu are main medium of instruction in all schools in rural as well as urban areas in the entire valley, Kashmiri is used partly, especially in rural areas and in the elementary classes. Our inquiry in this regard got the response noted in the Table 11

The Table 11 reveals that 33.31 per cent of schools [in which the children of our respondents] have the sole language of English as the medium of instruction. These missionary and private schools are urban-based and accommodate the children from upper-middle and upper classes. All these schools are non-governmental.

Table 11
MEDIUM OF INSTRUCTION IN THE SCHOOLS

S.No	Theme/Question	Respondents [district-wise]						Total
	What is medium of inst.	A	B	B	K	P	S	
	in your child's school?	No./%	No./%	No./%	No./%	No./%	No./%	No./%
1.	English	279 34.87	264 33.00	325 40.62	200 25.00	350 43.75	190 23.75	1599 33.31
2.	Urdu	190 23.75	165 20.62	235 29.57	390 48.75	300 37.50	280 35.00	1560 32.50
3.	Hindi	45 5.62	31 3.87	- -	- -	17 2.02	20 2.50	113 2.35
4.	Kashmiri	29 3.62	62 7.75	- -	10 1.25	- -	20 2.50	121 2.50
5.	N.A/N.R.	267 33.37	278 34.75	240 30.00	200 25.00	133 16.62	298 36.25	1408 29.33
	Total	800 100.00	800 100.00	800 100.00	800 100.00	800 100.00	800 100.00	4800 100.00

Second, 32.50 per cent schools have Urdu language as the medium of instruction. These are governmental and some private schools. Here English is also used partly. These schools accommodate the students from the middle classes.

Third, 2.35 per cent schools have Hindi as the medium of instruction. These are lesser in number and have been established by different communities like army schools, air force schools, Kendriya Vidyalayas, Sainik Schools and so on.

Finally, Kashmiri as the medium of instruction is used in some governmental and private schools in the rural areas.

6

Health Problems

6.1. Availability of Health Institutions and Facilities

In order to get an overview of the health institutions and facilities in all areas, we made the relevant inquiry. The information we received from this inquiry has been noted in the Table 1:

Table 1
HEALTH INSTITUTIONS AND FACILITIES AVAILABLE

S.No	*Theme/Question*		*Respondents [district-wise]*						*Total*
	Health Institutions and		*A*	*B*	*B*	*K*	*P*	*S*	
	Facilities available		*No./%*	*No./%*	*No./%*	*No./%*	*No./%*	*No./%*	*No./%*
Governmental:									
1.	D./SD Hospital	R	6	6	3	3	3	2	23
		U	4	4	7	3	7	8	33
2.	P.H.Cs.	R	146	130	141	100	121	80	718
		U	36	20	30	21	20	130	217

(Contd.)

(Contd. Table 1)

S.No	Theme/Question Health Institutions and Facilities available		Respondents [district-wise] A No./%	B No./%	B No./%	K No./%	P No./%	S No./%	Total No./%
	Non-Governmental:								
3.	Nursing Homes	R	01	-	-	01	-	02	03
		U	03	05	03	01	01	05	18
4.	Health Shops	R	25	15	10	12	15	10	87
		U	25	10	15	05	10	20	85
5.	Medical Shops	R	337	205	270	102	300	81	1295
		U	76	55	61	60	80	201	533
6.	Clinical Labor	U	32	22	10	3	8	80	155

The Table 1 conveys that there are significant number of hospitals, nursing homes, drug shops and clinical laboratories functioning in the valley. These statistical details may not correspond with the official figures or may not reflect the actual and existing number. In actuality, these figures represent the number conveyed by the respondents. Moreover, these numbers may not include those institutions and facilities which were closed/burnt in the last decade or were not functional at present. In essence, these numbers are indicative and shows the trend of providing the medical help.

6.2. Immunization of Children

One of the most crucial aspects of the health of children is related to the process of immunization within specific time-frame and with regular intervals. It is upheld that if children are given immunization dozes within specific time frame and at regular intervals, the normalcy of their health is ensured. If not, the normal growth of health of children is endangered.

Table 2
FUNCTIONING OF THE IMMUNIZATION PROGRAMMES

S.No	*Theme/Question*	*Respondents [district-wise]*						*Total*
	Have your children	*A*	*B*	*B*	*K*	*P*	*S*	
	Undergone immunization programme?	*No./%*	*No./%*	*No./%*	*No./%*	*No./%*	*No./%*	*No./%*
1.	Yes	468	470	490	350	567	460	2962
		58.50	58.75	61.25	47.75	70.87	57.50	58.43
2.	Courses: B.C.S.	468	470	490	350	567	460	2806
		100.00	-	100.00	100.00	100.00	100.00	100.00
	D.P.T.	468	470	490	350	500	460	2738
		100.00	00.00	100.00	100.00	100.00	100.00	100.00
	POLIO	468	470	490	350	500	460	2738
		100.00	-	100.00	100.00	100.00	100.00	100.00
	Measles	468	470	490	350	500	460	2738
		100.00	-	100.00	100.00	100.00	100.00	100.00
3.	No	65	42	70	250	100	50	470
		8.12	5.25	8.75	31.25	12.50	6.25	9.79
4.	N.A/N.R	267	288	240	200	133	290	1368
		32.37	36.00	30.00	25.00	6.62	36.25	28.50
	Total	800	800	800	800	800	800	4800
		100.00	100.00	100.00	100.00	100.00	100.00	100.00

Though the immunization-related health facility system had collapsed during the militancy, it has been revived partly in past few years. In this context, our inquiry about the functioning of immunization programmes got the information recorded in the Table 2.

The Table 2 reveals clearly that 2962/4800 [58.43 per cent] respondents had maintained regularity in getting immunization dozes for their children. This was more applicable in the urban areas than in the rural areas. This was partly because of the restoration of basic health facilities in the previous few years and partly because of increasing awareness about the immunization dozes of children. In this situation, more and more people are availing the immunization and other health care facilities for the children.

On the other hand, despite the availability of most of the facilities, 470/4800 [9.79 per cent] respondents had not availed any of the facility. This may be related to the factor of unawareness about the importance of immunization courses.

6.3. Common Diseases Among the Children

In order to know the actuality and pattern of diseases among children, it is necessary to find out about the common diseases which make the children [of that area] victims most often and with dreaded consequences. In this regard, the respondents were asked to identify the common diseases in which their children were trapped repeatedly in the last ten years or more. Their response has been noted in the Table 3.

The Table 3 conveys that significant proportion of children faced some particular diseases. While cough and cold was faced by 58.54 per cent, dysentery had caught by 61.70 per cent children of the respondents. Again, 41.00 per cent children were facing fever, malaria and jaundice, while 23.10 per cent children trapped in other diseases.

Table 3
COMMON DISEASES AMONG THE CHILDREN

S.No	Theme/Question	Respondents [district-wise]						Total
	Identify common diseases among Your children	A	B	B	K	P	S	
		No./%	No./%	No./%	No./%	No./%	No./%	No./%
1.	Cough and Cold	633	739	395	401	441	201	2610
		79.12	92.37	49.37	50.12	55.12	25.12	58.54
2.	Dysentery	712	659	460	471	500	100	2962
		89.00	82.37	57.50	58.87	70.00	12.50	61.70
3.	Children specific diseases	414	643	395	369	391	125	1968
		51.75	8.57	49.37	46.12	48.87	15.62	41.00
4.	Other diseases	195	160	171	271	192	120	1109
		24.37	20.00	21.37	33.87	74.00	15.00	23.10

We also inquired about the methods to be adopted for controlling these diseases effectively. While 65.31 per cent respondents emphasized on providing medical treatment and other necessary medical facilities to the children by the government, 34.69 per cent respondents stressed on providing pure drinking water and nutritious-balanced diet.

6.4. Pre-natal and Post-natal Care

Other crucial aspect of the birth and subsequent health of children is directly related to the pre-natal and post-natal care which their mothers take during the period of pregnancy. In this regard, our inquiry among the respondents got the response entered in the Table 4.

Table 4
PRE-NATAL AND POST-NATAL CARE BY RESPONDENTS

S.No	*Theme/Question*	*Respondents [district-wise]*						*Total*
	Have you taken pre-Natal & post-natal care ?	*A*	*B*	*B*	*K*	*P*	*S*	
		No./%	*No./%*	*No./%*	*No./%*	*No./%*	*No./%*	*No./%*
1.	Yes	413 51.62	480 60.00	460 57.50	31 39.50	547 68.37	340 42.50	2556 53.50
2.	Where? Public H.C.	283 68.52	365 76.04	400 86.95	299 94.62	510 93.23	150 44.11	2007 78.82
3.	Private H.C.	130 120	115 82	60 100	17 284	37 120	190 50	549 756
4.	No	120 15.00	82 10.25	100 12.50	284 35.50	120 15.00	50 6.25	756 15.75
5.	N.A/N.R.	267 33.37	238 29.75	240 30.00	200 25.00	133 16.62	290 36.25	1368 28.50
	Total	800 100.00	800 100.00	800 100.00	800 100.00	800 100.00	800 100.00	4800 100.00

The Table 4 reveals that majority of respondents, 2556/4800 [53.25 per cent] had taken pre-natal and post-natal care. It seems that [among these respondents] while 76.52 per cent had availed these facilities at public health centres [of the govt.] mostly in the villages, 21.47 per cent had taken this care in the private health centres mostly located in the urban areas. While the former category of respondents had taken the health care partly, the latter category had taken full medical care.

On the other hand, 756/4800 [15.75 per cent] respondents had not taken pre-natal and post-natal care. The reasons responsible for this behaviour were that either the respondents were not aware about this care or [if they were aware partly or fully] they were not in a position to pay for it. Again, in most of the cases, these medical facilities were not available in their rural areas.

6.5. Conduct of Delivery

In the traditional society of Kashmir, the delivery was usually conducted by the Dai who was only person available for the purpose. They used to get no professional training for conducting delivery. So, their conduct of delivery involved major risks such as death of the mother or the baby. But, a lot of change has occurred now. In the present situation, number of professionals with specific training and expertise are available. But, still some people, particularly in the rural areas, engage non-professionals for conducting delivery. Our inquiry on this problem gave us the information noted in Table 5.

The Table 5 reveals that in the cases of about 59 per cent [20.66. 4.09 and 34.62 per cent] respondents, persons with some professional training conducted delivery. On the one hand, this reflects a significant degree of positive change that ensured the safe birth of more and more children. On the other hand, this situation reduced the heavy human cost in terms of reducing the high rate of death at birth. Thus the traditional mortality rate was controlled partly.

Table 5
CONDUCT OF DELIVERY

S.No	*Theme/Question*	*Respondents [district-wise]*						*Total*
	Who conducted last delivery in your family?	*A*	*B*	*B*	*K*	*P*	*S*	
		No./%	*No./%*	*No./%*	*No./%*	*No./%*	*No./%*	*No./%*
1.	Doctor	93 11.62	80 10.00	100 12.50	20 2.50	100 12.50	599 74.87	992 20.66
2.	A.N.M.	23 2.87	32 .00	39 4.87	10 1.25	41 5.12	50 6.25	195 4.09
3.	Trained Dai	350 43.75	384 48.00	370 6.25	130 16.25	268 46.00	60 7.50	1662 54.62
4.	Untrained Dai	94 11.75	64 8.00	61 7.62	360 45.00	71 8.87	51 6.37	701 14.60
5.	Relative	160 20.00	163 20.37	140 17.50	190 23.75	130 16.25	30 3.75	813 1.73
6.	Neighbour	80 10.00	77 9.62	90 11.25	90 11.25	90 11.25	10 1.25	437 9.10
	Total	800 100.00	800 100.00	800 100.00	800 100.00	800 100.00	800 100.00	4800 100.00

The table also conveys that in the cases of 41 per cent [14.60, 16.93 and 9.10 per cent] respondents, the traditional practices related to the conduct of delivery still continue. This continuity involves the significant human cost in terms of death at birth thus contributing to higher mortality rate.

6.6. Place of Delivery

Traditionally, the delivery used to take place at home, which was considered an ideal place for it. This practice involved certain risks, including the death of child at birth. However, with the overall improvement in the life conditions, this practice too has undergone radical change. With the increase in the number of hospitals and other health centres and relevant facilities, more and more people get encouraged to take their women to the hospitals and other health centres at the time of delivery, where they got all required facilities. Our investigation reveals this trend of change and can be seen in the Table 6.

Table 6
PLACE OF DELIVERY

S.No	*Theme/Question*	*Respondents [district-wise]-*						*Total*
	Where your last-	*A*	*B*	*B*	*K*	*P*	*S*	
	delivery took place?	*No./%*	*No./%*	*No./%*	*No./%*	*No./%*	*No./%*	*No./%*
1.	Hospital	93	80	100	20	100	599	992
		11.62	10.00	12.50	2.50	12.50	87.37	20.66
2.	Private Nursing Home	30	86	50	10	50	30	256
		3.75	10.75	6.25	1.25	6.25	3.75	5.33

(Contd.)

(Contd. Table 6)

S.No	Theme/Question	Respondents [district-wise]						Total
	Where your last-delivery took place?	A	B	B	K	P	S	
		No./%	No./%	No./%	No./%	No./%	No./%	No./%
3.	Home	677	634	650	710	650	171	3552
		84.62	79.25	81.25	96.25	81.25	21.37	74.00
	Total	800	800	800	800	800	800	4800
		100.00	100.00	100.00	100.00	100.00	100.00	100.00

The Table 6 reveals that 992/4800 [200.66 per cent] respondents or their family members had delivered their last child in the hospitals in the city of Srinagar and other towns. These hospitals are government hospitals and are located in Srinagar city and district towns in the Kashmir valley.

Second, 256 [5.33 per cent) respondents or their family members had delivered the last child in the private nursing homes located mainly in the Srinagar city. These respondents generally belonged to the upper and middle classes.

Third, the huge majority of 3552/4800 [74.00 per cent] respondents or/and their family members had delivered their previous child in their homes, but with a difference. It means that the delivery was conducted at home by the concerned doctor or trained *Dai* or any other expert person.

6.7. Number of Children

The previous sections makes it clear sufficiently that significant improvement has taken place in the existing health conditions which have effected our respondents. This situation was characterized by two main features. First, the availability of medical facilities has improved a lot. Second, there seems heavy increase in the utilization of these medical facilities in rural as well as urban areas. Both these factors together have contributed to the life to increasing number of children at or after birth. This is important development in the context in which a significant per cent of children were dying at the time or immediately after their birth. Our investigation in this field divulged the information noted in the Table 7.

Table 7
PLACE OF DELIVERY

S.No	*Number of Children Survived in the family [average]*	*Respondents [district-wise]*						*Total*
		A	*B*	*B*	*K*	*P*	*S*	
		No./%	*No./%*	*No./%*	*No./%*	*No./%*	*No./%*	*No./%*
1.	No. of children born:							
	-Total	2.5	4	3.6	4	3.8	3	3.5
	-Male	1.5	2	2	2	2	1	1.7
	-Female	1	2	1.6	2	1.8	2	1.7
2.	No. of children Living:							
	-Total	2	3.5	3	3	3	2.5	2.8
	-Male	1	1.6	2	2	1.4	1	1.4
	-Female	1	1.6	1	1	1.6	1.5	1.2
3.	No. of children dead:							
	-Total	0.5	0.5	0.6	1	0.8	0.5	1
	-Male	0.5	0.2	0.0	0.0	0.6	0.0	0.2
	-Female	0.0	0.4	0.6	1	0.2	0.5	0.4

The Table 7 shows increase in crude births in comparison with the past. So, we may infer that while child birth rates have increased tremendously, the child death rates have reduced simultaneously. It follows that the infant mortality rate has also been reduced considerably. We may also say that these trends of population growth may continue in the near future.

6.8. Views about Having More Children

In the traditional situation, the common wish was to have more number of children, especially the male ones. In that situation, high birth rates were matched with high death rates. This type of situation had a dual impact. First, the birth to a large number of children with lesser gaps had effected negatively the health of the concerned women. Second, it led to the heavy increase in the population. In this background, we carried out an investigation regarding the opinion of our respondents regarding having more number of children. Their response has been recorded in the Table 8.

The Table 8 reveals that a large scale change regarding the attitude and behaviour related to having more number of children in the family. Thus a small number of 197/4800 [4.10 per cent] respondents expressed their willingness to have more children. When these respondents were asked to mention the exact number of children, they would like to add to their existing families, they showed the response as follows:

(a) 1 child — 60.19 per cent respondents
(b) 2 children — 26.39 per cent respondents
(c) 3 and more children — 11.16 per cent respondents

Table 8
WISH TO HAVE MORE NUMBER OF CHILDREN

S.No	Theme/Question		Respondents [district-wise]						Total
	Do you want to have more children?		A No./%	B No./%	B No./%	K No./%	P No./%	S No./%	No./%
1.	Yes		20 2.50	32 4.00	25 3.12	80 10.00	30 3.75	10 1.25	197 4.10
2.	Number	1	14 70.00	16 50.00	20 80.00	50 62.50	15 50.00	5 50.00	123 60.19
		2	3 15.00	9 28.12	5 20.00	20 25.00	10 30.33	5 50.00	52 26.09
		3	3 6.00	7 21.87	- -	10 12.50	5 16.66	- -	22 11.16
3.	Sex:	Male	18 90.00	24 75.00	18 72.00	56 70.00	15 50.00	5 50.00	61 69.13
		Female	2 10.00	8 25.00	7 28.00	24 30.00	15 50.00	5 50.00	61 30.76
4.	No.		513 64.12	480 60.00	535 6.87	500 65.00	637 79.82	500 62.50	3235 63.39
5	N.A/N.R.		267 33.37	288 36.00	240 30.00	20 28.00	133 16.62	290 36.25	1368 28.50
	Total		800 100.00	800 100.00	800 100.00	800 100.00	800 100.00	800 100.00	4800 100.00

On the other hand the dominant majority of 3235/4800 [67.39 per cent) respondents said a categorical "no" to the question. This is the result of the cumulative impact of the processes of modernization going on in the Kashmiri society in the last five decades. There is a feeling among the respondents that such an attitude and behaviour may increase in future.

6.9. Effects of Having More Children

It has been established in the scientific research that there are certain negative implications on the health of women as well as children for having large number of children, especially when there is no or less gap between the birth of children. This was also conveyed by a large number of respondents. Details in this regard can be seen in the Table 9.

Table 9
EFFECT OF HAVING MORE CHILDREN

S.No	*Theme/Question*	*Respondents [district-wise]*						*Total*
	Has more no. of children effected your health adversely?	*A*	*B*	*B*	*K*	*P*	*S*	
		No./%	*No./%*	*No./%*	*No./%*	*No./%*	*No./%*	*No./%*
1.	Yes	463	480	500	450	577	500	2990
		57.87	60.00	62.50	56.25	74.62	62.50	62.29
2.	No	70	64	60	150	70	10	424
		8.75	8.00	7.50	18.75	8.75	1.25	8.83

(Contd.)

(Contd. Table 9)

S.No	Theme/Question	Respondents [district-wise]						Total
	Has more no. of children effected your health adversely?	A	B	B	K	P	S	
		No./%	No./%	No./%	No./%	No./%	No./%	No./%
3.	N.A/N.R.	267	256	240	200	133	290	1386
		33.37	32.00	30.00	25.00	16.62	36.25	28.87
	Total	800	800	800	800	800	800	4800
		100.00	100.00	100.00	100.00	100.00	100.00	100.00

The table reveals that the majority of 2990/4800 [62.39 per cent] respondents had faced negative implications of their health mainly due to the birth to a large number of children. They also felt that these implications are increasing day by day. Moreover, there has been increasing awareness about these negative implications of giving birth to more children.

On the other hand, only 424/4800 [8.83 per cent] respondents felt that they were not effected badly due to giving birth to a large number of children. But, at the same time, they were not fully sure about it.

6.10. Immediate Response to the Illness

Like in other parts of India, the illness is also responded or treated here by going to the priest or by worshipping the gods and goddesses. This still happens in extreme traditional families or extreme traditional situations. But, the widespread impact of the processes of modernization has reduced considerably these practices. People now go to the doctor or use medicines for curing themselves. In this context, we made a relevant inquiry. The response which we received portrays in the Table 10.

Table 10

IMMEDIATE RESPONSE/TREATMENT TO THE ILLNESS

S.No	Theme/Question	Respondents [district-wise]						Total
	What do you do	A	B	B	K	P	S	
	when you fall ill?	No./%	No./%	No./%	No./%	No./%	No./%	No./%
1.	Go to the Priest	51	50	71	100	50	21	343
		6.37	6.25	8.87	12.50	6.25	2.62	7.14
2.	Go to the medicine shop	331	350	311	310	350	378	2030
		41.37	43.75	38.87	38.75	43.75	47.25	42.29
3.	Go to the P.H.C	290	300	280	340	300	201	1711
		36.25	37.50	35.00	42.50	37.50	25.12	35.64
4.	Go to the Doctor	128	100	138	50	100	200	716
		16.00	12.50	17.75	6.25	12.50	50.00	14.91
	Total	800	800	800	800	800	800	4800
		100.00	100.00	100.00	100.00	100.00	100.00	100.00

The Table 10 portrays four types of behaviour of the respondents when they fall ill. First, a significant group of 2030/4800 [42.29 per cent) respondents go to the medicine shop and get the medicines from any person there, when they fall ill. The persons give all medicine to the people, even without seeing the doctor's advice slip. It is because the Drug Act has not been applied in the J&K state. This situation has led to the extreme abuse of drugs in the state.

Second, a significant number of 1711/4800 [35.64 per cent] respondents visit the local PHE when they fall ill. The PHE provides partial or complete treatment depending upon the availability of expert doctors, relevant facilities and the required drugs.

Third, a small group of 716/4800 [14.91 per cent] respondents consult the doctor immediately after they fall ill. This mostly happens in the urban areas where doctors, facilities and medicines are easily available.

Last, a tiny group of 343/4800 [7.14 per cent] respondents go to the priest in their locality to get relief from the disease. While some get relief with this spiritual treatment, others consult the doctors after they don't get the relief from the priest's spiritual treatment.

6.11. Visit to the Local PHC

It has generally been observed that not all people visit the local P.H.C. when they fall ill, though these centres exist and function there. It depends upon the health culture of the family. On the other hand, some people visit the local PHC regularly. These people usually belong to the lower and lower-middle classes which take maximum benefit from the centres. In this context, we investigated about the pattern of visits of the people to their local PHC at the time of their illness, and got the response noted in the following Table 11.

Table 11
VISIT TO THE LOCAL PHC

S.No	Theme/Question		Respondents [district-wise]						Total
	How many times you Visit local PHC?/ Period		A	B	B	K	P	S	
			No./%	No./%	No./%	No./%	No./%	No./%	No./%
1.	In 1 last month	01	251	259	200	202	250	160	1322
			31.37	32.37	25.00	25.25	31.25	20.00	27.50
		02	168	160	30	36	169	140	703
			21.00	20.00	3.75	4.50	31.12	17.50	14.64
		03	61	80	50	52	40	100	393
			7.62	10.00	6.25	6.50	6.25	12.50	8.18
		None	320	301	520	510	331	400	2362
			40.00	37.62	65.00	63.75	41.37	50.00	49.62
2.	In last 1 year	01-05	347	352	312	300	341	125	1777
			43.37	44.00	39.00	37.50	42.62	15.60	37.02
		06-10	290	304	261	273	296	130	1554
			36.25	38.00	32.62	34.12	37.00	16.25	32.37
		11-15	83	64	21	29	80	120	397
			10.37	8.00	2.62	3.62	10.00	15.00	8.27
		16& +	49	54	16	20	51	125	315
			6.12	6.75	2.00	2.50	6.37	15.52	6.56
		None	31	26	190	198	33	300	778
			3.87	3.25	23.75	24.75	4.12	37.50	16.20

The Table 11 reveals that 1322/4800 [27.54 per cent] respondents have visited the local PHC once in a period of one month for self treatment or treatment of the family member/s, while 703/4800 [14.64 per cent] respondents visited the FHC in the same period and for the same period.

Finally, a tiny group of 393/4800 [8.18 per cent] respondents have visited the local PHC for three or more than three times. On the other hand, a significant number of 2382/4800 [49.62 per cent] respondents had not visited the local PHC at all. Most of them go to private clinics or expert. doctors for treatment of their or their family member's treatment.

The same response with little difference was found among the respondents during the period of one year. While 1777/4800 [37.02 per cent] respondents have visited the local PHC for 1 - 5 times, 1554/4800 [32.37 per cent] respondents have done the same for 6 - 10 times in the last one year. A significant number of 778/4800 [16.20 per cent] respondents had not visited the PHC any time in the same long period.

In the light of all above findings, there emerge some basic questions regarding the scope and relevance of the PHC.

6.12. Breast Feeding of Children

The practice of breast feeding is medically considered must for the normal and desirable growth of children. But, in the situation of overall change in which women remain busy for earning money or remain out of home for most part of the day, this practice was stopped partly or wholly. As a result of this development, children suffered in the field of health. In this context, the inquiry about the breast feeding of children gave the information indcluded in the Table 12.

The Table 12 reveals that a significant group of women in the valley has emerged which has stopped partly or fully the practice of breast feeding. This group is composed of the women who usually work outside their homes for most part of the day. But, the majority of 50.77 per cent respondents still continue with the practice of breast feeding of their children, though some among them are working women.

Table 12

PRACTICE OF BREAST FEEDING OF CHILDREN

S.No	*Theme/Question*	*Respondents [district-wise]*						*Total*
	Do you breast feed	*A*	*B*	*B*	*K*	*P*	*S*	
	your children?	*No./%*	*No./%*	*No./%*	*No./%*	*No./%*	*No./%*	*No./%*
1.	Yes	500	512	500	600	667	-	3349
		62.50	64.00	70.00	75.00	83.37	63.75	50.77
2.	No	33	-	-	-	-	-	-
		4.12	-	-	-	-	-	19.68
3.	N.A/N.R.	267	288	240	200	133	290	1418
		33.37	36.00	30.00	25.00	16.62	36.25	29.54
	Total	800	800	800	800	800	800	4800
		100.00	100.00	100.00	100.00	100.00	100.00	100.00

6.13. Awareness about Family Planning

There is a general feeling among respondents that all of them are aware about positive aspects of the family planning programme. This is because of the cumulative effect of many social, economic, educational, demographic and other relevant factors. Among other crucial implications, it keeps the health of women normal and stable in this background, our inquiry about the awareness among women regarding family planning gave the information noted in Table 13.

Table 13

AWARENESS ABOUT FAMILY PLANNING PROGRMMES

S.No	Theme/Question	Respondents [district-wise]						Total
	Are you aware of Family Planning Programmes?	A	B	B	K	P	S	
		No./%	No./%	No./%	No./%	No./%	No./%	No./%
1.	Yes	610	572	566	491	580	752	4233
		76.25	71.50	70.30	61.15	72.50	94.00	88.18
2.	No	190	228	234	307	220	48	567
		23.75	28.50	29.70	28.25	27.50	6.00	4.81
	Total	800	800	800	800	800	800	4800
		100.00	100.00	100.00	100.00	100.00	100.00	100.00

The above table conveys clearly that a dominant majority of 4233/4800 [88.18 per cent] respondents were fully aware about the family planning programmes. Some among them had used the family planning devices. On the other hand, a minority of 567/4800 [11.81 per cent] respondents showed their unawareness from family planning programmes. Most of them are illiterate and live in rural areas.

6.14. Use of Family Planning Methods

In continuation of the previous section's theme, we investigated about the methods used by our respondents for family planning, i.e. birth control. In this regard, we got the information recorded in the Table 14.

Table 14
USE OF FAMILY PLANNING METHODS

S.No	Theme/Question	Respondents [district-wise]						Total
	Which family plann.	A	B	B	K	P	S	
	method you used?	No./%	No./%	No./%	No./%	No./%	No./%	No./%
1.	I.U.D/C.U.T	33 4.12	64 8.00	50 6.25	20 2.50	30 3.75	100 1.50	297 6.18
2.	Oral Pills	460 57.50	456 52.00	480 60.00	400 50.00	600 75.00	400 50.00	2756 58.25
3	Condom	40 5.00	42 5.25	30 3.75	50 6.25	37 4.62	10 1.25	209 4.35
4.	N.A/N.R.	267 33.67	239 34.75	240 30.00	310 41.25	133 16.62	290 36.25	1488 31.00
	Total	800 100.00	800 100.00	800 100.00	800 100.00	800 100.00	800 100.00	4800 100.00

The Table 14 reveals that the oral pill method is common among the respondents which was reported by 2756/4800 [58.15 per cent] among them. IUD/CUT and condom methods come at second and third number as was reported by 6.18 and 4.35 per cent respondents respectively. On the other hand, 1488/4800 [31.20 per cent] respondents showed unawareness, which has to be taken seriously and treated accordingly.

7

Discrimination Problems

7.1. Harressment of Working Women

In the traditional situation, women used to work within' their homes. But, in the changing situation when women got formal education, they developed their role outside their homes. So, they had to work in office for the whole day. In this situation, while they got many benefits, they had to face certain problems too. One such problem is the harassment of working women by men at their places of work. In this background, our inquiry got the response noted in the Table 1.

Table 1
HARASSMENT OF THE WORKING WOMEN

S.No	*Theme/Question*	*Respondents [district-wise]*						*Total*
	Where you harassed at your place of work?	*A*	*B*	*B*	*K*	*P*	*S*	
		No./%	*No./%*	*No./%*	*No./%*	*No./%*	*No./%*	*No./%*
1.	Yes	10 1.25	30 3.75	25 20.00	50 6.25	10 20.00	50 16.66	175 22.17

(Contd.)

(Contd. Table 1)

S.No	Theme/Question	Respondents [district-wise]						Total
	Where you harassed at your place of work?	A	B	B	K	P	S	
		No./%	No./%	No./%	No./%	No./%	No./%	No./%
2.	No	49 6.12	135 16.67	100 80.00	50 6.75	40 80.00	250 83.33	614 79.82
3.	Total	59 100.00	155 100.00	125 100.00	100 100.00	50 100.00	300 100.00	789 100.00

The Table 1 divulges that a dominant majority of 614/789 [79.82 per cent] respondents were not harassed by their superiors or colleagues at their places of work. But, at the same time, a significant portion of working women, i.e. *175/789* [22.17 per cent], reported that they are harassed by colleagues and superiors at their places of work. This is a new trend which has serious implications for women at large.

7.2. Harassment of Working Women: Nature and Offenders

In the preceding section, it became clear that a significant portion of women was harassed at their places of work. It seems important to know about the nature of harassment and the persons involved in this offence against working women. A relevant investigation was carried out and this information was recorded in the Table 2.

The Table 2 shows clearly that a major portion of the working women face extreme type of harassment at the hands of their officers and colleagues at their places of work. While 53.10 per cent respondents faced mental harassment, 38.18 per cent among

Table 2
HARASSMENT OF WORKING WOMEN:NATURE & OFFENDERS

S.No	Theme/Question	Respondents [district-wise]						Total
	Harassment of	A	B	B	K	P	S	
	working women	No./%	No./%	No./%	No./%	No./%	No./%	No./%
1.	Nature: Physical	5	10	10	20	3	15	63
		50.00	33.33	40.00	40.00	30.00	30.00	38.18
	Mental	5	15	10	30	3	30	93
		50.00	50.00	40.00	60.00	30.00	60.00	53.14
	Other types	-	5	5	-	4	5	19
		-	16.46	20.00	-	40.00	10.00	10.85
	Total	10	30	25	50	10	50	175
		100.00	100.00	100.00	100.00	100.00	100.00	100.00
2.	By Whom: Officers	3	15	10	30	3	20	81
		30.00	50.00	40.00	60.00	30.00	20.00	46.28
	Colleagues	7	15	15	10	7	20	74
		70.00	50.00	60.00	20.00	70.00	40.00	42.28
	Others	-	-	-	10	-	10	20
		-	-	-	20.00	-	20.00	11.42
	Total	10	30	25	50	10	50	175
		100.00	100.00	100.00	100.00	100.00	100.00	100.00

them faced physical harassment. 10.85 per cent respondents reported that they faced other kinds of harassment which includes teasing on petty matters.

On the other hand, it was reported that officers carried out harassment against their subordinate women in 46.28 per cent cases, while colleagues of equal status did the harassment in 42.28 per cent cases.

It follows that in majority of the cases, mental harassment of working women at their places of work took place by officers followed by physical harassment by officers and colleagues.

7.3. Harassment of Working Women: Complaints and Action

In continuation of the theme of harassment of working women, an inquiry was made about the reaction which the concerned women had shown after the incident [of harassment]. The concerned women were asked whether they made the complaint to the authority against the harassment. It yes, was the expected action against the offenders taken? This inquiry gave us the response as shown in the Table 3

Table 3
HARASSMENT OF WORKING WOMEN:COMPLAINT AND ACTION

S.No	*Theme/Question*	*Respondents [district-wise]*						*Total*
	Have you made complaint against harassment?	*A*	*B*	*B*	*K*	*P*	*S*	
		No./%	*No./%*	*No./%*	*No./%*	*No./%*	*No./%*	*No./%*
1.	Yes	5	10	-	-	5	10	30
		50.00	33.33	-	-	50.00	20.00	1.14
2.	Result-Satisfactory	-	5	-	-	5	5	15
		-	50.00	-	-	50.00	50.00	50.00

(Contd.)

(Contd. Table 3)

S.No	*Theme/Question*			*Respondents [district-wise]*				*Total*
	Have you made	*A*	*B*	*B*	*K*	*P*	*S*	
	complaint against harassment?	*No./%*	*No./%*	*No./%*	*No./%*	*No./%*	*No./%*	*No./%*
	-Not satisfactory	5	5	-	-	-	05	15
		100.00	50.00	-	-	-	50.00	50.00
3.	No	05	20	25	50	05	40	145
		50.00	66.66	100.00	100.00	50.00	80.00	82.85
4.	Resons:							
	-Don't want to highlight	-	10	15	20	5	30	80
		-	50.00	60.00	40.00	100.00	75.00	55.17
	-to avoid reaction	3	5	-	20	-	5	33
		60.00	25.00	-	40.00	-	12.50	22.75
	-to avoid discrimination	2	5	10	10	-	05	32
	in future	40.00	25.00	40.00	20.00	-	12.50	25.51

The Table 3 shows while 17.14 per cent respondents had complained to the authorities against the cases of harassment at their places of work, the majority of 82.85 per cent respondents had not dared to complain against the offenders. In the former case, 50.00 per cent respondents were satisfied about the action taken by the concerned authorities against the offenders, an equal number of respondents, i.e. 50.00 per cent, were not satisfied on the action taken against the offenders.

On the other hand, 82.85 per cent respondents did not register any complaint against the offenders for three specific reasons which are as follows:

(a) Don't want to highlight the incident 55.17 per cent
(b) To avoid extreme reaction 22.75 per cent
(c) To avoid discrimination in future 25.51 per cent

7.4. Discrimination in the Wage Payment

There is a general impression that all women workers are discriminated in all cases related to wages and their payment. This seems not wholly correct. Our probe in this regard gave us the information noted in the Table 4:

Table 4
DISCRIMINATION IN WAGES PAID TO THE WOMEN

S.No	*Theme/Question*	*Respondents [district-wise]*						*Total*
	have you got lesser	*A*	*B*	*B*	*K*	*P*	*S*	
	wages than men?	*No./%*	*No./%*	*No./%*	*No./%*	*No./%*	*No./%*	*No./%*
1.	Yes	25	55	25	25	-	100	230
		42.37	35.48	20.00	25.00	-	33.33	29.15
2.	No	34	100	100	75	50	200	559
		57.62	62.50	80.00	75.00	100.00	66.66	70.84
3.	Total	59	155	125	100	50	300	789
		100.00	100.00	100.00	100.00	100.00	100.00	100.00

The Table 4 clearly reveals that while a significant group of working women, 29.15 per cent respondents were facing discrimination in terms of getting lesser wages than their male counterparts, the majority of 70.84 per cent respondents gave theopposite response. It seems that the latter respondents were working in government offices where the chances of discrimination are least. On the other hand, the former respondents worked in the private sector which is completely unorganized and unprotected.

7.5. Complaint Against Lesser Wages to Women

The previous sections clearly establish :he point that significant number of working women respondents get lesser wages than their male counterparts. This happens mainly in the private and unorganized sector. It has been observed that there is less scope for complaint against the authority concerned. Even if they make a complaint, it is not taken seriously leading to no major difference in the actual situation. Our probe in this regard gave us the information included in the Table 5.

Table 5

COMPLAINT AGAINST LESSER WAGES TO WOMEN

S.No	*Theme/Question*	*Respondents [district-wise]*						*Total*
	Have you complained	*A*	*B*	*B*	*K*	*P*	*S*	
	against lesser wages?	*No./%*	*No./%*	*No./%*	*No./%*	*No./%*	*No./%*	*No./%*
1.	Yes	25	55	00	20	00	20	120
		10.00	00	00	80.00	00	20.00	52.17
2.	Results: Pay revised	10	43	00	10	00	10	73
		40.00	78.00	00	50.00	00	50.00	60.83
	No response	15	12	-	10	-	10	47
		60.00	23.81	-	50.00	-	50.00	60.83

(Contd.)

(Contd. Table 5)

S.No	Theme/Question	Respondents [district-wise]						Total
	Have you complained	A	B	B	K	P	S	
	against lesser wages?	No./%	No./%	No./%	No./%	No./%	No./%	No./%
3.	No.	-	-	25	5	-	80	110
		-	-	100.00	20.00	-	80.00	47.82

The Table 5 shows that 52..17 per cent working women respondents had complained to the authorities concerned against the lesser salary, while 47.82 per cent respondents had not dared to complain. It was also revealed that out of the total complaints, the salary was increased in the 60.83 per cent cases, while no action was taken in 39.16 per cent cases. On the other hand, 47.82 per cent working women respondents had registered no complaint because they felt nothing will come out. It may lead to antagonism which will endanger their services. So, they remain silent and their suffering continues.

7.6. Working Women in Handicraft Sector

There are no census reports or other correct estimates available about the exact number of women working in different fields of handicraft sector. In order to know the number of women working in the handicraft sector, we carried out a relevant inquiry. The responses have been noted in the Table 6.

The Table 7 reveals that women work in significant numbers in most of the fields of the handicraft sector. While most of them work in significant numbers in the fields of *shawlbati*, crevel work and *kaleenbafi*, others in lesser proportion work in other fields.

Table 6
WOMEN WORKING IN HANDICRAFT SECTOR

S.No	*Theme/Question*	*Respondents [district-wise]*						*Total*
	Working in the	*A*	*B*	*B*	*K*	*P*	*S*	
	handicraft sector	*No./%*	*No./%*	*No./%*	*No./%*	*No./%*	*No./%*	*No./%*
1.	Yes	302	233	420	100	200	210	1465
		100.00	100.00	100.00	100.00	100.00	100.00	100.00
	Area : Shawlbati	63	50	310	15	80	30	548
		2080	21.45	73.80	15.00	40.00	14.28	37.40
	Kaleenbati	54	110	50	20	20	20	274
		17.88	47.21	·11.90	20.00	10.00	9.52	18.70
	Phum weaving	70	35	10	05	30	50	201
		23.12	15.45	2.38	5.00	15.00	23.80	13.72
	Blanket weaving	45	4	10	10	10	20	99
		14.90	1.71	2.38	10.00	5.00	9.52	6.75
	Paper Machine	17	15	-	-	05	40	32
		5.62	6.40		-	2.50	19.04	2.59
	Wood Carving	23	15	-	-	-	-	32
		7.61	6.49	-	-	-	-	2.59
	Crevel work	30	3	40	50	55	50	228
		9.50	1.28	9.25	50.00	27.50	23.00	-

7.7. Discrimination Against Women in Handicraft Sector

As has been mentioned in preceding sections, women are consciously discriminated partly hi all sectors/fields. But, in the handicraft sector, they get more discriminated comparatively. In addition to the exploitation by middlemen and wholesalers/ exporters, women working in the handicraft sector face discrimination at the same hands in terms of lesser wages. Our probe in this connection divulged the information entered in the Table 7.

Table 7
DISCRIMINATION AGAINST WOMEN IN THE HANDICRAFT SECTOR

S.No	Theme/Question	Respondents [district-wise]						Total
	Do you get equal	A	B	B	K	P	S	
	[to men] wages?	No./%	No./%	No./%	No./%	No./%	No./%	No./%
1.	Yes	33	43	40	31	100	170	777
		14.16	14.23	95.23	31.00	50.00	80.95	53.03
2.	No	200	259	20	69	100	40	688
		85.83	85.43	4.76	69.00	50.00	19.04	46.96
	Total	233	302	420	100	200	210	1465
		100.00	100.00	100.00	100.00	100.00	100.00	100.00

The Table 7 reveals that while 777/1465 [53.03 per cent] respondents got equal (to men] wages for their handicraft work,

688/1465 [46.96 per cent] respondents didn't get equal (to men] wages for their work. In the case of latter group of respondents, the discrimination W3S made possible through manipulation, exploitation and the situation in which there are not fixed wages for different items of handicrafts. In the case of former group of respondents, though they feel they get equal wages, they too get exploited.

7.8. Discrimination Against Women in Inheritance Rights

Like in other areas of life, women get discriminated in practice in getting fully their inheritance rights granted to them in the Islamic *shariat*. In the past, it was a common practice, especially in the rural areas. However, in the present situation, this practice has changed radically in rural as well as urban areas. Our inquiry in this connection gave the information recorded in the Table 8.

Table 8
DISCRIMINATION AGAINST WOMEN IN INHERITANCE RIGHTS

S.No	*Theme/Question*	*Respondents [district-wise]*						*Total*
	Are you discriminated	*A*	*B*	*B*	*K*	*P*	*S*	
	in inheritance rights?	*No./%*	*No./%*	*No./%*	*No./%*	*No./%*	*No./%*	*No./%*
1.	Yes	320 40.00	502 62.75	410 51.25	350 43.75	100 50.00	100 12.50	2082 43.37
2.	No	270 33.75	189 23.62	255 31.87	250 31.25	200 25.00	600 75.00	1764 36.75

(Contd.)

(Contd. Table 8)

S.No	Theme/Question	Respondents [district-wise]						Total
	Are you discriminated	A	B	B	K	P	S	
	in inheritance rights?	No./%	No./%	No./%	No./%	No./%	No./%	No./%
3.	N.A/N.R	210	109	135	200	200	100	954
		26.25	13.62	16.87	25.00	25.00	12.50	19.87
	Total	800	800	800	800	800	800	4800
		100.00	100.00	100.00	100.00	100.00	100.00	100.00

The Table 8 shows while 2082/4800 [43.37 per cent] respondents were given due inheritance rights, 1764/4800 [36.75 per cent] respondents were denied these rights partly or wholly. While the former response reflects the change in the relevant practice, the latter response represents the degree of continuity in the traditional practice. It seems that, in the present day situation, while the practice of denial of inheritance rights to daughters/women is reducing, the practice of the payment of .inheritance rights is increasing.

7.9. Religion and Discrimination Against Women

As the discrimination against women goes on, it is justified by parents on the basis of religion. They argue that since Islam considers women unequal, she gets discriminated in several fields and at several occasions. But, this argument is contested by other parents. The argue that since women in Islam is considered not unequal but a different person than men, they have got different [from men] set of rights and obligations. In this context, we asked the women respondents do they feel discriminated in their religion. Their reply has been noted in the Table 9.

Table 9

RELIGION AND DISCRIMINATION AGAINST WOMEN

S.No	*Theme/Question*	*Respondents [district-wise]*						*Total*
	Do you feel discriminated by religion in inheritance?	*A*	*B*	*B*	*K*	*P*	*S*	
		No./%	*No./%*	*No./%*	*No./%*	*No./%*	*No./%*	*No./%*
1.	Yes	100	227	50	75	200	370	1022
		12.50	28.37	6.25	9.39	25.00	46.25	21.29
2.	No	500	385	710	625	424	330	2984
		62.50	48.18	88.75	79.37	53.00	41.25	62.16
3.	N.A/N.R	200	188	40	90	176	10	794
		25.00	23.00	5.00	11.25	22.00	11.50	16.56
	Total	800	800	800	800	800	800	4800
		100.00	100.00	100.00	100.00	100.00	100.00	100.00

The Table 9 reveals that 1022/4800 [21.39 per cent] respondents felt religion provides the base for discrimination against women in inheritance rights while 2984/4800 [62.16 per cent) respondents felt in the opposite way. The later group of women upheld the view that religion has provided due share to women, but it is denied to them in practice by the followers of the religion. Moreover, this practice goes in violation and not in consonance with religion.

7.10. Laws Against the Women Interests

Like religion, some laws too go against large interest of women. This is what some women believe. They demand that since these discriminatory laws have no social approval, these must be dropped or revised. They consider it necessary for the emancipation of all women. In this context, we made an inquiry about the existing laws which hurt the women's interests. The respondents response reflect in the Table 10.

Table 10
LAWS AGAINST THE WOMEN'S INTERESTES

S.No	Theme/Question	Respondents [district-wise]						Total
	Do some laws hurt	A	B	B	K	P	S	
	you Interests?	No./%	No./%	No./%	No./%	No./%	No./%	No./%
1.	Yes	59	109	71	45	112	307	703
		7.37	13.62	8.87	5.62	14.00	38.37	14.67
2.	No	542	525	528	546	488	393	3032
		67.75	66.87	66.00	68.25	61.00	49.12	63.16
3.	N.A/N.R	199	156	201	209	200	100	1065
		24.87	19.50	25.12	26.12	25.00	12.50	22.19
	Total	800	800	800	800	800	800	4800
		100.00	100.00	100.00	100.00	100.00	100.00	100.00

The Table 10 reveals that while 703/4800 [14.64 per cent] respondents did say that some existing laws stand against the women's interests, 3032/4800 [63.16 per cent] respondents felt in the opposite way. The former group of respondents upheld that the discriminatory laws must be scrapped and replaced by the progressive legislation.

When they were asked to cite these discriminatory laws, while majority of the respondents referred to the Islamic *sharia* or Muslim Personal laws such as lesser share in the parental property, lesser weightage to women witnesses, right to divorce to the men only, and denial of the inheritance to the wife after her husband dies [if his father is alive], minority of the respondents could not refer to any law which discriminates them. The former and latter responses can be explained in terms of literacy and illiteracy of respondents respectively.

7.11. Authority of Women

The social status of a person reveals in the authority which he or she holds in the family and the society at large. If the social status of a person is low, his/her authority also stands low and limited. On the other hand, if the status of a person is high, his/her authority stands high and unlimited relatively. Traditionally, the women in Kashmir had low authority within and outside family. But, the processes of social transformation at large have changed the traditional pattern of authority held by women. In the changing situation in Kashmir, women increased as well as intensified their authority in many areas such as control over property, daily decision-making, marriage of children, children's education and construction of new house. In order to know the exact authority of women in very crucial areas, we made a relevant inquiry, whose results have been recorded in the Table 11.

Table 11
NATURE OF THE AUTHORITY OF WOMEN

S.No	*Theme/Question*		*Respondents [district-wise]*						*Total*
	Authority of Women		*A*	*B*	*B*	*K*	*P*	*S*	
			No./%	*No./%*	*No./%*	*No./%*	*No./%*	*No./%*	*No./%*
1.	Control over property	M*	800	800	800	800	800	800	4800
			100	100	100	100	100	100	100
		F							
		B	-	-	-	-	-	-	-
			-	-	-	-	-	-	-
2.	Daily Decision-making	M	200	660	690	700	600	400	3340
			25.00	82.50	86.25	87.50	86.25	50.00	69.58
		F	100	140	110	10	10	200	670
			12.50	17.50	13.75	1.25	2.75	25.00	13.95
		B	500	-	-	90	-	200	790
			62.50	-	-	11.25		25.00	16.45
3.	Marriage of children	M	410	609	510	410	510	200	2648
			51.25	76.00	63.75	51.25	67.75	25.00	55.16
		F	50	32	40	50	40	200	412
			6.25	4.00	5.00	6.25	5.00	25.00	8.58
		B	340	160	250	390	250	400	1740
			42.50	20.00	31.25	42.50	31.25	50.00	36.25
4.	Money Investment	M	610	576	700	610	576	400	3472
			76.25	72.00	87.50	74.25	72.00	50.00	36.25

(Contd.)

(Contd. Table 11)

S.No	*Theme/Question*		*Respondents [district-wise]*						*Total*
	Authority of Women		*A*	*B*	*B*	*K*	*P*	*S*	
			No./%	*No./%*	*No./%*	*No./%*	*No./%*	*No./%*	*No./%*
		F	20	64	10	20	64	200	378
			2.50	8.00	1.25	2.50	8.00	25.00	7.87
		B	170	160	90	170	160	200	950
			31.25	20.00	11.25	21.50	20.00	25.00	19.79
5.	Children's Education	M	600	624	450	600	600	411	3309
			75.00	78.00	56.25	75.00	75.00	51.33	68.33
		F	51	32	60	51	32	310	536
			6.37	4.00	7.50	6.37	4.00	28.75	11.16
		B	149	144	290	149	144	89	965
			19.62	18.00	26.25	18.62	8.00	11.12	20.10
6.	Construction of new house	M	690	544	710	690	700	391	3725
			86.25	68.00	88.75	86.25	89.50	48.87	77.80
		F	10	-	20	10	10	209	259
			1.25	-	2.50	1.25	1.25	26.12	5.39
		B	100	256	70	100	90	200	816
			12.50	32.00	8.75	2.50	11.25	25.00	17.00

*M = Male F = Female B = Both

7.12. Discrimination Against Girl Child

Like their mothers, sisters and .other elder women, the girl children too are discriminated in all economic sectors. When this information was sought from the women respondents, they provided it as portrays from the Table 12.

Table 12
DISCRIMINATION AGAINST GIRL CHILD

S.No	*Theme/Question*	*Respondents [district-wise]*						*Total*
	Do your girl child	*A*	*B*	*B*	*K*	*P*	*S*	
	face discrimination?	*No./%*	*No./%*	*No./%*	*No./%*	*No./%*	*No./%*	*No./%*
1.	Yes	203	128	330	400	203	95	1359
		25.37	16.00	41.25	50.00	25.37	11.87	28.31
2.	No	497	592	395	310	497	610	2901
		62.12	74.00	49.37	29.75	63.13	76.25	60.43
3.	N.A/N.R	100	80	75	90	100	95	540
		12.50	10.00	9.39	11.25	12.05	11.87	11.25
	Total	800	800	800	800	800	800	4800
		100.00	100.00	100.00	100.00	100.00	100.00	100.00

The Table 12 conveys that a significant number of girl children of the respondents,1359/4800 [28.31 per cent] were facing discrimination. This is what was felt by 28.31 per cent of our women respondents. These girls were working in different sectors, especially handicrafts.

7.13. Abortion of Female Fetus

Among several undesirable practices performed by women themselves. the abortion of female fetus stands as a distinctive practice. It is generally believed that women opt for this inhuman practice non-voluntarily than voluntarily. In fact, it is held that women do this barbarian job under compulsion. But, the actual situation portrays a different picture, see Table 13.

Table 13
ABORTION OF FEMALE FETUS BY WOMEN

S.No	Theme/Question	Respondents [district-wise]						Total
	Should women go for abortion of female fetus?	A	B	B	K	P	S	
		No./%	No./%	No./%	No./%	No./%	No./%	No./%
1.	Yes	201 25.12	49 6.12	110 3.75	210 25.25	201 25.12	100 12.50	871 18.14
2.	No	389 48.62	211 37.26	290 36.25	90 1.25	389 8.62	600 75.00	1969 41.16
3.	N.A/N.R	410 51.05	540 67.50	400 50.00	500 62.50	410 51.25	100 12.50	2360 49.16
	Total	800 100.00	800 100.00	800 100.00	800 100.00	800 100.00	800 100.00	4800 100.00

The Table 13 reveals that while 871/4800 [18.14 per cent] women respondents favour the abortion, the significant group of 1969/4800 [41.02 per cent] women respondents oppose it strongly on ethical and religious grounds. It is important to note less than 14 per cent women respondents provide one or the other explanation for going for this inhuman practice. It is immaterial to say that they do it under compulsion or pressure on the part of males as well as females in the in-laws family.

8

CONCLUSION

1. It has been established in the previous chapters that women in the Kashmir valley generally lived in extreme traditional situation till the dawn of 20 century. The life of women in that society was characterized mainly with dependency, inequality, discrimination, harassment, economic suffering, total ignorance and so on.

2. However, the earlier decades of the 20th century experienced the formal initiation of the broader and deeper process of transformation in the total situation related to the problems of women. The triggering factors were indigenous and exogenous. While the former refers to the political, ideological, social and religious factors at national and international level at that time, the latter points toward the economic, cultural, educational and other related factors.

3. After 1947, in the state of Jammu and Kashmir, several governments irrespective of their political and ideological differences, carried out several efforts to follow the broader objective of the improvement of women's situation. Other

efforts in the educational, economic, social and health fields were carried out in the previous few decades by the NGOs. It is important to note here that all these governmental as well as non-governmental efforts could not prove fruitful and effective fully mainly because of the continuous political instability and political conflict in the state.

4. However, the cumulative effect of various formal and informal measures created a situation in which

   (a) women at large came out of the extreme traditional situation;

   (b) women adopted consciously a significant degree of positive change;

   (c) women developed a new role which they asserted in different fields of life; and

   (d) women socialized the new generation/s for their new role and status in the broader society.

5. The crucial fact related to the change among women in the contemporary times in Kashmir is that this was not total, qualitatively or quantitatively. It necessarily means that only certain, and not full, degree of change was adopted by the women. It also means that change in one field of life was not concomitantly followed in other fields. In refers to a situation in which all changes at the ideational level were not systematically followed at the behavioural level. In actuality, it created a situation in which modernity was adopted partly and, at the same time, the tradition was maintained partly.

6. The women's situation, mentioned above, reflected in all five areas of investigation carried out by us. The relevant details follows:

(a) Though most of the ideas related to social transformation were adopted fully, all its implications were neither accepted nor implemented. Thus the new role of working women was accepted by all, but its implications were not shared by the family members. While they are denied the economic independence, they are harassed at their places of work.

(b) Though the idea of education to all, irrespective of sex difference, was accepted and emphasized by all, the girl children are discriminated in pursuing higher education and drop-outs.

(c) While majority of women work in the agriculture and handicraft sectors, minority of them have developed working women role by working in service and business sectors. Moreover, their self-earned money is not allowed to be spent on her and by her alone.

(d) Though a dominant majority of women is fully conscious about the medical treatment, especially before, during and after delivery, very less number of them take the needed/required treatment: Moreover, despite having awareness about the health culture, not many women maintain it.

(e) Though majority of women stand educationally advanced, economically prosperous, socially forward and culturally exposed, they practise/allow the practice of their discrimination. This practice is not only inter-sex but intra-sex phenomenon.

7. The portrayal of women's situation above reveals clearly that women in Kashmir pass through the process of transformation. All available evidence shows that this process will continue and mature. In this grand process, while the tradition gets reduced, modernity gets enlarged. The direction of this macro-level process is towards change, development and emancipation. Thus the women in Kashmir is in transition.

9

Sugesstions

A. Social Problems

1. As has been mentioned in the relevant section in this report, the practice of dowry prevails in Kashmir with a difference, i.e. the parents of the girl pay dowry more on the insistence of the girl. In terms of financial implications, this practice makes hardly any difference for the parents. So, this trend stands undesirable and needs to be opposed and eradicated. While relevant social legislation aimed at banning the practice of dowry can play its role, a strong social movement needs to be initiated for negating the practice of dowry.

2. The amount of *mahr* must be fixed at the time of marriage according to the economic status of the groom. He must also be in a position to pay it. This fixed amount should be paid fully *as* per the Islamic laws which suggest its full payment at that time. The payment should neither be paid in parts nor deferred in any way. Violation of these practices should be stopped forcefully and social

legislation may be initiated in this regard. On the other hand, wider social consciousness must be raised in favour of the total amount of *mahr* to be paid at the time of marriage.

3. The practice of polygamy has to be seen in proper perspective. It has been permitted not ordered to marry more than one woman for solid reasons. Moreover, certain conditions have to be fulfilled before marrying more than one woman. The conditions include that the man can do justice with all wives and has strong financial base. Though there are very less number of polygamous marriages, care should be taken to discourage it. Both, social legislation and social action may be used for this purpose.

4. The occurrence of divorce is negligible in the valley. But, the trend is emerging and increasing as well. So, the practice of divorce has to be negated and controlled. Emphasis must be on projecting divorce as the last resort and an undesirable act as characterized by the Prophet. Social and legal measures have to be carried out in this regard. Social legislation should be formulated and enforced against the misuse of polygamy and legal measures have to be carried out in this regard. Social legislation should be formulated and enforced against the misuse of polygamy and divorce as has been done in several Muslim countries.

5. Remarriage of the divorced women must be encouraged and helped. In this regard, formulating the necessary social legislation will prove of tremendous help. At the

same time, widespread social approval and mobilization are also needed.

6. Women must be allowed to inherit all due property from all sources. Islam grants the woman a specific share in the parents' and husband's property. It must be ensured that these shares are actually received by women. In this regard, while the existing customary laws in Kashmir must be negated, the Muslim Personal laws must be applied. Violation of women's rights is needed to be stopped fully.

7. The problems related to marital adjustment must be takan seriously and must be resolved in the ational-realistic framework. The facts of the emergence of working women's coal role must be accepted whole heatedly. Following that, an equitable and reciprocal relationship must be established between wife and husband on the one hand and between the woman and all family members.

8. The problems of working women can be dealt with at two level. At the societal level, the newly emerged role of the working women must get social approval/ recognition. It will take care of many problems which the working women face inside as well as outside their homes. At the formal-legal level, many problems of women, especially harassment, discrimination and violation of women's rights, can be minimized or resolved at their places of work.

9. The problems related to the dual role of women and its crucial implications may be resolved in rational-social framework. Within the home, the husband and other

family members must provide supportive roles. They can be helpful in the problems related to day take-care and socialization of children, deviance and control within the family. Outside their homes, the working women have to develop a new perception of problems, which will relieve them from many tensions.

10. The wife-beating [and husband-beating too] stands as the most inhuman practice. It must be stopped immediately. While the govemment can play certain role in this regard, the society at large has to eradicate it completely.

B. Economic Problems

1 The women's role in agriculture, handicrafts, small business and household occupations must be highlighted, emphasized and analysed. It is because the portrayal of women's role will divulge the importance of their role in different sectors of economy. A!l this will certainly contribute in establishing gender equality.

2 Majority of women workers work in the traditional sectors/ fields of economy. Now they should be thrown in new sectors/fields of economy such as service and small business. They should be made very crucial in the total economy and economic reconstructicn in the Kashmir valley. Moreover, women's economic/occupational mobility must contribute to their psychological and social development in totality.

3. Women's work inside as well as outside their homes must be valued in market/material terms. The women

must be oriented towards their work accordingly. While every work performed by women must be paid, the domestic work must be explained in these terms, if not paid.

4. Women must be paid for every work they perform except for the household work. This will lead to the economic independence of women. It follows that women will eam themselves and will spend themselves according to their preferences and priorities. They will also spend for self needs and/or family needs as the situation demands.

5. Women working in different occupations, especially the world-famous handicrafts, must be paid equally to that of their male counterparts for every work they perform. This must be ensured through the legal means. At the same time, social mobilization is needed for giving equal treatment to the women's work.

6. Standard wages for all standard works, especially in the handicraft fields/sectors, must be fixed according to the relevant and standard criteria. In this direction, the government, in cooperation with the concerned people and their associations/organizations, has to determine wages of all major and minor items and has to enforce these set wages. Violations have to be dealt seriously.

7. The maximum degree of exploitation of women goes on in the handicraft sector. This has to be stopped completely or reduced considerably, necessarily and immediately. The exploitation of the girl children has to be the special focus of all formal and informal actions.

8 The mass exploitation in the handicraft sector/fields can be stopped or reduced through fixing standard rates of all handicraft items, enforcing these wages seriously and sincerely by the concerned agencies, regular checking of regular and full wages to the women workers, maintaining the standards of all items, and opening credible outlets for the products of the women workers. At the same time, wider social consciousness must be raised against the on-going exploitation.

9 The government and non-governmental organizations and agencies must work systematically for establishing independent centres and co-operatives for educated as well as uneducated women. While these organizations and agencies will provide financial base for women's centres and co-operatives, these will help in their maintenance and will open outlets for the produced items.

10. All desirous educated unemployed women in rural as well as urban areas must be helped financially by the government and non-governmental agencies to establish their own independent units in various economic sectors/ fields.

11. Women Working in Unorganized sector must be organized by their women trade union movement. This seems necessary for safeguarding all rights of women like the women workers in the organized sector.

12. The rural women deserve special allention on the part of governmental and non-governmental organizations

and agencies. They also deserve special measures to protect their rights in totality and to ensure equal treatment in all areas, especially economic.

C. Educational Problems

1. Since women's literacy rate stands very low [as low as 10 per cent] in the Kashmir valley, all governmental as well as non-govemmental efforts must concentrate on improving the situation in this field. Target-oriented and time-bound programmes must be initiated and pursued seriously. It is surprising that a state which had free education from primary till university could not allain desirable levels of literacy during the last fifty years.

2. In the absence of 1991 census records, all estimates and other assumptions regarding women's literacy seem partial and particularistic. These figures do not convey the real/actual situation. So, there emerges an important need for carrying out scientific-empirical surveys and studies on all aspects of women's literacy.

3. The government must provide all necessary educational facilities to all, especially to the female children and at the primary-secondary level. These facilities include school buildings, qualified teachers, libraries, laboratories and so on. The finances must be provided for these facilities on priority basis even if the budgetary provision has to be increased for this purpose. This financial allocation may prove real investment for future human 'resource development'.

4. The government must encourage systematically the primary education to women. At the same time, the objective of education to all as early as possible must be pursued vigorously. While the government must provide all necessary financial support in this compaign, the women at large must be mobilized to pursue education seriously and get benefited to the maximum extent.

5. It is important to establish the pro-literacy environment for the cause of women's education. This will emerge as the 'social input' in the process of educational advancement of women. In actuality, a strong social movement for women's educational advancement will prove of tremendous help in this regard.

6. The drop-out of children, especially of female sex, must be necessarily checked in forrmal and informal ways. Formally, the governmental and non-govemmental efforts,specially providing the necessary financial support, will certainly reduce the drop-out rate, especially at the elementary stage. Informally, social consciousness may be raised against the drop-out at the elementary and secondary stages.

7. The cost of education in the government schools must be reduced considerably. There should be absolute reducation in the tuition fee and other dues. Heavy admission fee in private/missionary schools must be abolished. Moreover, children belonging to the weakest economic classes/groups must be exempted from paying the fee and dues.

8. The government schocls must be made the centres of attention and excellence in primary and secondary school level education. These schools have more children, lesser fee and other dues, qualified.trained staff, more funds available and maximum facilities. Using all these, the govemment needs to make these schools functional and productive.

9. The role of private schools particularly of those which have been established by the Christian missionaries long back, has been recognized in the process of educational advancement. These schools may continue to function to spread modem education, but they should not exploit the people by demanding large amounts of money at the time of admission and other dues later on. They should provide the better and quality education without hurting the government schools.

10. Since many schools were burnt/destroyed during the militancy, necessary facilities such as school buildings, fumiture and furnishing, scientific equipment, libraries and laboratories must be provided on priority basis.

D. Health Problems

1. The health institutions must be established in all areas as per the population needs. Simultaneously, all necessary facilities, especially related to women, must be provided in these institutions. The health institutions and facilities must be made available in the far off villages.

2. Full immunization of infants must be ensured. In this regard, while the govemment has to provide the

professional manpower and medicines, the positive social response has to be offered by the broad-based social acceptability. Thus the relevant programmes may prove highly effective and productive as well.

3. In the context of health problems of women, the public health centres must be provided with expert doctors, particularly female doctors, necessary medicines, equipment and other crucial facilities. If these have been already provided, these must be utilized to the maximum possible extent to benefit the masses.

4. It is very important that all hospitals/health centres at the district, tehsil, block and village levels must be provided with medicines, services and facilities required by women at the time of delivery of babies. The priority must start from the town in this regard. Moreover, necessary medicines, facilities and services required for pre-natal and post-natal care must necessarily be made available during day and night. The services of expert doctors and the transport mast be available all during 24 hours.

5. The awareness regarding medical care before, during and after the delivery must be developed through all possible means, especially print and electronic media. The women studying in higher classes, i.e. colleges and universities, must be provided this information through the syllabi. Very less care must be taken about the taboos in this regard. But, at the same time, vulgarised and immoralized information must not be allowed to flow in the society.

6. The common diseases of women existing in the valley must be identified and their dimensions and implications

observed through the scientific research.Subsequently, the relevant and needed strategy, schemes and programmes [in the short-term and long-term planning] must be carried out to control and to eradicated these diseases. The eradication of these diseases can be made a reality in the framework of preventive care and curative care. While the former refers to adopt preventive long-term measures by the concerned women, the latter means immediate medical treatment by the concerned women provided by the governmental as well as non-governmental agencies.

7. In general, the women in the valley must be made aware about approaching/observing diseases scientifically. In other words, it means that women [and others too] must develop and maintain the health culture. Among other features, it also refers to consume necessary and balanced diet, to avoid medically undesirable works and things, to contact the expert doctor at the time of falling ill, and to allow the doctor's advice in totality.

8. A strong and widespread compaign must be carried out to emphasize the point that any serious and physiological disease must be got treated by the expert doctor in the P.H.Cs, hospitals and clinics and going to the priest at the initiation of disease may prove disastrous. Thus this practice must be strongly condemned. If the treatment of the priest is necessary, it must be done after the doctor's treatment of the disease.

9 In order to stop widespread abuse of drugs in the valley, the Drug Act must be implemented in the entire state. It will necessarily stop the undesirable side-effects

and help to develop a habit to use drugs when needed by a person.

10. The establishment of private clinics and nursing homes in the valley must be appreciated. But, at the same time, the government must ensure that these health institutions provide standard services to the people. Special care must be taken of the financial aspect, i.e. wages of medical and para-medical staff and changes for the treatment of various diseases and operations. In brief, the proprietors of these health institutions must not be allowed to exploit the people.

11. Specific measures must be taken to control the mortality rates, especially at the time of or immediately after the birth of children. While the concerned facilities and services can be provided in the hospitals, women must be aware to take relevant measures in this regard.

12. The strong social compaign for adopting family planning measures by the women is already going on. It must be further expanded, strengthened and made intensive. The print and electronic media must continuously portray the positive implications of the adoption of several measures of family planning. The themes related to the family planning must also be made part of syllabi in the higher classes of women.

13. Breast feeding must be presented as the ideal practice for feeding the child by mother in the earlier period. Focus of the compaign must be on working women. Social mobilization can prove more effective than the

government orders/actions in this regard. So, voluntary social action is highly needed in this regard.

E. Discrimination Problems

1. Broadly, the problems of discrimination can be dealt at two levels. At the governmental level, all necessary legislation and its implementation related to the gender discrimination must be carried out. At the societal level, while social consciousness has to be raised against various practices of gender discrimination, a strong social movement has to be started to safeguard all rights of women and to ensure equal treatment of women within and outside their families.

2. The practice of gender discrimination must be made the priority item in the social, political, economic and other agenda of all political and social organizations. This ideal must be pursued irrespective of the political and ideological differences between various political parties.

3. The ideal of gender equality can be achieved by empowering women at all levels and in all areas. This basic process of fundamental social transformation must start from the family and affect even the composition of members of parliament in the country. In fact, without empowering women in the family, how can we empower them in the broader society. So, the entire society must be engulfed in to this process.

4. However, the women too have to be responsive towards other members and groups in society and family. In other

words, they have to be reciprocal in their social relationship, especially within their families. If women's new role and status is approved by others in the family and society, they too have to accept their obligations towards them.

5. Harassment of women at their places of work has to be stopped formally and forcefully. All rules and laws must be used to punish those who take the chance to harass the women. At the same time, all formal and informal efforts must be carried out to establish the social ethos within and outside the work places in which women will be respected and not mal-treated.

6. The problems of the girl child must be specifically focussed.in order to divulge more information about the nature of their suffering. A lot of scientific-empirical research must be sponsored to know the existing situation of these children. Subsequently, the governmental and non-governmental efforts must be initiated to improve their life conditions in Kashmir.

7. Abortions must not be allowed to carry out, except in unavoidable cases, on ethical grounds. Abortion of female fetus to kill the female baby must be portrayed as a heinous crime against humanity. While it must be formally banned by the law of the land, the concerned women must be organized/prepared to oppose this practice. Moreover, a widely representative social movement must work to ensure that women [and men too] must never agree to go for this practice.

10

Report of the Workshop

1. It may be argued sociologically that women in the traditional society of Kashmir were usually discriminated maltreated, as was the case in all traditional societies. They remained dependent on men throughout their lives in economic as well as non-economic fields.

2. But, this situation started undergoing the process of deeper and wider transformation from the early decades of this century. The major factors responsible for this macro-level change among women included political consciousness, modern education, cultural awareness, economic conditions and social awakening.

3. However, a fact of basic importance stands that this transformation among women in Kashmir had benefited them primarily because its direction was towards their emancipation. But, at the same time, the change gave rise to a new set of problems in the changing social dynamics.

4. Thus, it may be argued that, in the last five decades, though women's condition in Kashmir improved considerably, they had to face a new set of problems in

many fields of life. In actuality, these problems may be considered the necessary co-relates and unavoidable implications of the broader social transformation.

5. It was essentially in the preceding context that we carried out a detailed empirical investigation to identify and analyse crucial problems which the women faced in Kashmir. This study was carried out by 25 research investigators in 1998-1999 in all districts of the Kashmir province. The study's focus was on the following areas:

   - social problems
   - economic problems
   - educational problems
   - health problems
   - problems of discrimination

6. The study concentrated on the representative sample of 4,800 women respondents [i.e. 800 respondents from each district] who were selected on the basis of variables like age, income, occupation/profession, literacy, religion, rural urban affiliation and other social categories. After the empirical investigation was over, a detailed draft report was prepared.

7. It was essentially in the context of the Survey Report that a workshop was organized on the suggestion of the Ministry of Statistics and Programme Implementation, New Delhi. This workshop was organized on 11-12 November 1999 at Gandhi Bhawan, University of Kashmir, Srinagar. The participants included academicians, social welfare planners-administrators, experts in Women

Studies, women activists, research scholars and students. While the workshop was inaugurated by the [Acting] Vice Chancellor of University of Kashmir, Professor Abdul Wahid, Professor A. A. Ali, famous academician-educationist of Kashmir was the Chief Guest at the workshop.

8. The two-days workshop had five sessions in total. The first Inaugural session was held on 11 November 1999 [Thursday] at 11.00 a.m. First, Professor B. A. Dabla, Chief Organizer, delivered the welcome address, in which he gave the background, need and objectives of the workshop and welcomed all out-station and in-station guests. Second, Dr. R. N. Pandey and Mr. Harish Chandra, representing the Ministry of Statistics, New Delhi. Dr. Pandey, who was the Monitoring Officer of the survey, gave details about his visits to the valley to monitor and supervise the survey investigation. He showed extreme satisfaction with the commendable work carried out by Professor Dabla and his team in minimum possible time. He emphasized the need to carry out further research on the topics related to this survey and his ministry may provide the necessary help in this regard.

9. Third, Professor Abdul Wahid [Acting] Vice-Chancellor, appreciated the efforts of the Department of Sociology, especially of its Head, Dr. Dabla, for carrying out research on crucial and need-based topics. He said that the present survey about women's problems in Kashmir is rich in content and can be of tremendous help in the planning and implementation of women's welfare programmes.

10. Fourth, Professor A. A. Ali congratulated the Department of Sociology, especially its Head, Professor B. A. Dabla, for this pioneering research work on Kashmir. It will serve not only the academic purpose, but cause of women's development in Kashmir. He emphasized the point that empowerment of women is must for the overall development of human society. This process must start necessarily from the family where we must provide them all facilities and ensure all of their rights.

At the last, Mrs. Aneesa Shafi and Dr. Khurshidul Islam presented the vote of thanks on the part of the organizers of the workshop.

11. After a brief tea break, the second session started at 12.30 and it was chaired by Professor A. A. Ali. In this important session, two review [of survey] presentations were made by Professor A. G. Madhosh and Professor Fayaz Ahmad. The former made the following core points:

-the sample of the survey is very less as it represents 0.13 of the total women's population in the Kashmir province;
-there seems disproportionate representation to rural and religious compositions;
-the cost of education for children seems ambiguous and it needs clarity;
-the drop-out rates for female age-groups needs further elucidation;
-in general, the survey stands first of its kind in Kashmir, for which Dr. Dabla and his team must be congratulated.

12. The second review presentation was made by Prof. Dost Mohammad. Some of the arguments which he made are as follows:

-the survey reflects very hard and excellent effort on the part of Dr. Dabla and his team. This macro-level research must be followed by micro-level research on the part of other scholars;

-economic field needs further probe in order to get data on more crucial areas;

-the problems of old-age and delayed marriage must also be considered as core problems of women;

-the practice of dowry has to be observed in the relative context of Kashmir.

This was followed by discussion and comments and suggestions were made. These revolved around the topics such as representative character of sample, rural/ urban basis, methodology and objectives of the survey, nature of gender discrimination, educational enrolment and drop-out rate of female students, and payment of *mahr* and dowry. Finally, Professor Ali concluded the discussion by saying that though women's problems are crucial for total development of society, their problems need scientific investigation and solution as well. In this context, Dr. Dabla work stand trend setting.

13. The third session started at 2.45 p.m. under the chairmanship of Professor Dost Mohammad. Two review

presentations by Professor Fayaz Ahmad and Professor M. A. Qadri were made in this session. Professor Fayaz Ahmad made the following central arguments:

-the survey carried out by Dr. Dabla and his team of sociologists represents a comprehensive study of women's problems in Kashmir. It is highly commendable work for us as such a study has not been carried out here.

-the emerging role of working women needs further research especially related to its implications vis-a-vis children and old age and on family at large;

-in the context of technological and Electronic revolution, the role of women within and outside their homes needs reassessment; and

-the human development is comprehensive and all encompassing concept. The women's development must be seen, in this broader perspective.

14. The second review presentation was made by Professor M. A. Qadri. Some of his main arguments were as follows:

-the concept of dowry in Kashmir needs further clarification as it involves legal offence here;

-the practices related to the payment of *mehr* needs micro-level studies as most of these violate the Shariah law;

-the incidence of wife-beating seems more than has been shown in the survey report;

-there seems no law existing in the country which goes explicitly against women [as was reported by some women respondents]; and
-the survey stands as a quality piece of social science research, for which Dr. Dabla must be appreciated.

This was followed by a discussion which revolved around the topics which included the following:

-methodology for the survey;
-divorce and remarriage in Kashmir;
-wife-beating in Kashmir;
-women's rights and inheritance laws;
-economic independence of women;
-drop-out rates;
-widows and orphans conditions; and
-islamic concepts regarding women's role in the society.

Finally, Professor Dost Mohammad concluded the session by saying that the survey findings seem highly realistic and representative. However, further scientific research must be carried out for deeper and wider understanding of women's problems in Kashmir. At the last, Dr. R. N. Pandey and Dr. B.A. Dabla made some clarification about several points raised by the participants.

15. The fourth and fifth sessions were held together on 12 November 1999 at 11.00 A.M. and were presided over

by Professor M. A. Qadri. Dr. A. Shafi presented a sociologist's review of the survey. The review gave the holistic and theoretical framework for the realistic understanding of various problems of women. This was followed by a brief discussion. After this, Dr. B. A. Dabla made a detailed presentation and responded to all comments, suggestions, criticism and inquiries. He also agreed to incorporate relevant suggestions and comments in the text of the revised report. The discussion was concluded by the chairman by saying that this type of research must continue. Despite several crucial problems prevailing in the valley, Dr. Dabla has been able to carry out this quality piece of research. This is an example of academic commitment.

16. In the concluding session, Dr. Dabla explained the details of deliberations of two-days workshop. He maintained that, taking in to consideration the objectives, the workshop proved a grand success. He thanked all for the success of the workshop.

11

Working Women in Unorganized Sector

Context

01. In the broader and deeper processes of social change and development, all groups, communities and classes in the society face their implications partly or wholly and positively or negatively. In this changing dynamics, women in the Indian society too underwent a role and status inside as well as outside their homes. The emergence of the working role of women in the urban areas in India reflects this type of change among them. In this process of transformation, women in all parts of India were benefited in general. This pattern of change reflects in economic, social, political, cultural and educational fields.

02. But, at the same time, the women faced negative implications too. This phenomenon among women may be explained in terms of the emergence of several problems inside as well as outside their homes. In actuality, these problems are the after-effects of the adoption of the working role by them.

03. Thus the working women in Kashmir too faced a lot of problems primarily because of the adoption of the new working role

or the working career by them. It is important to note that while the working women in organized/sectors faced lesser problems comparatively, the working women in the unorganized sector experienced more problems than the former.

04.This theme in the Kashmir context was observe, analyzed and explained in 1990 by the author in a project study which was sponsored by the University Grants Commission, New Delhi. That study was based on an extensive fieldwork of 200 relevant respondents in the Kashmir valley working in many fields of the handicraft sector.

05. After about five years of period, the author felt the need to expand the framework of study and to update it. The expansion of the study meant the inclusion of more working women in the sample, inclusion of more areas in the handicraft sector, and increasing the number of variables, and so on. This expansion necessitated due to various developments which have taken place in the valley during the last five years, it had a direct impact in increasing and intensifying the problems of the working women in the unorganized handicraft sector.

06. Thus a study was carried out among two hundred women workers in unorganized handicraft sector in the Kashmir valley during the first half of the year 1996. The focus was on those working women who suffer more and on fields/sectors where the degree of exploitation was more. Moreover, the focus was on dimensions related to identifying the real socio-economic conditions, nature and degree of exploitation, and analysis of the crucial problems of the working women in unorganized handicraft sector.

Objectives

This study was aimed at to follow the below-mentioned broader objectives:

(i) to identify and explain the real socio-economic conditions of the working women in various unorganized handicraft sectors in the Kashmir valley;

(ii) to observe and assess the existing socio-economic conditions and problems of the working women in various unorganized handicraft sectors in the Kashmir valley; and

(iii) to provide suggestions for short-term and long-term planning/programmes/schemes aimed at to solve these crucial problems of the women working in different fields of the handicraft sector/s

Methodology

01. The methodology adopted in the previous study was continued in this study with some minor changes. The background and extra information was collected from secondary sources such as books, journals, articles, magazines, newspapers, films and so on.

02. The primary source information was collected through the techniques of Questionnaire and interview. While the questionnaire was given to the literate respondents (who filled it with the help of the investigator), the response of illiterate respondents was recorded in the format by the investigator. The latter response was possible through the interview of the respondents. The Questionnaire composed of 18 Questions (with each having Borne sub-Questions) of fixed-choice as well as of open-choice.

03. The sample composed of 200 respondents belonging to social, economic, educational, demographic, age, occupational and other categories. All respondents belonged to the rural and urban areas

Sample of Respondents

Age Groups	*Rural/ Urban*	*Income Groups*	*Field-1*	*Field-2*	*Field-3*	*Field-4*	*Total*
6-15 Years	Rural	I	3	4	3	4	14
	"	II	3	2	3	3	11
	"	III	-	-	-	-	-
	Urban	I	3	4	3	4	14
	"	II	3	2	3	3	11
	"	III	-	-	-	-	50
16-25 years	Rural	I	3	4	3	4	14
	"	II	3	3	2	3	11
	"	III	-	-	-	-	-
	Urban	I	3	3	3	4	13
	"	II	3	3	3	3	12
	"	III	-	-	-	-	-
26-40 years	Rural	I	4	3	3	3	13
	"	II	3	3	3	3	12
	"	III	-	-	-	-	-
	Urban	I	3	3	4	3	13
	"	II	3	3	3	3	12
	"	III	-	-	-	-	-

(Contd.)

(Contd. Table)

Age Groups	*Rural/ Urban*	*Income Groups*	*Field-1*	*Field-2*	*Field-3*	*Field-4*	*Total*
41 years	Rural	I	3	3	3	4	13
and above	"	II	3	3	3	3	12
	"	III	-	-	-	-	-
	Urban	I	4	3	3	3	13
	"	II	3	3	3	3	12
	"	III	-	-	-	-	-
Total			50	50	50	50	200

Field-1 - Carpet Weaving
Field-2 - Paper-machie
Field-3 - Shawl-bafi
Field-4 - Phum-Shahtosh weaving
- Namda-Blanket weaving

Income Groups: I : Rs. 2000/- and less
II : Rs. 2001/- to Rs. 5000/-
III: Rs. 5001/- and above.

of district Sri Nagar in the state of Jammu and Kashmir. This representative sample of respondents is shown in the following table (see the table on the next page).

04. After the information/data was collected, it was cumulated and tabulated. This practice enabled to explain and analyse the information gathered from the respondents. This also helped in arriving at certain conclusions in the sociological and scientific framework.

Findings

1. Work at Home or Centre

1.1. In the Kashmir valley, women working generally in the handicraft sectors generally work at their homes. However, in the previous few decades, these women and their girls have started working in Out-home handicraft centres which are either government sponsored or private sponsored. Our investigation revealed that the women in Kashmir work in both types of centres. The following table give information in this regard:

TABLE 1
WOMEN WORKING AT HOME OR IN THE CENTRES

S.No.	*Place of Work*	*Number*	*Per cent*
1.	At Home	125	62.50
2.	In the Centre:		
	- Government-sponsored	15	7.50
	- Private-sponsored	60	30.00
3.	Any other place	-	-
	Total	200	100.00

Our investigation revealed that 62.50 per cent of our sample respondents were working for different handicraft works at their homes. In fact, there is a tradition here that women in all handicraft sectors mostly worked at home. This suited them,especially during the winter season.Other factors which suit this type of work included that women feel relaxed and easy while working at home; women do the household jobs (such as cooking, washing and cleaning) and take care of their children simultaneously; and women work according to the time available to them. In this type of situation, while the concerned women do the handicraft work for earning money, they also feel at home. On the other hand, 37.50 per cent of our respondents (i.e. 75 out of the total of 200) worked in the out-home centres established either by the government or private individuals who are usually middlemen or wholesalers in the handicraft business at the national or international level. This trend of working in out-home centres is relatively new developed in the previous few decades.

This development coincided with the increasing demand for Kashmiri handicrafts in national and international markets. These centres have been established in their own or neighbouring localities of the concerned women. So, they have not to go to far off places for work. In these centres, women generally got comparatively more and regular wages. In the total of 75 respondents, while 15 respondents worked, government-owned centres, 60 respondents worke in privatly owned centres. While privately-owned centres were established earlier, the government started these centres in the previous few decades. In fact, there was a boom of these centres during 1970s and 1980s, when the state government took a big initiative to introduce these in every locality in the rural as well urban areas. This governmental effort with monetary benefits to the workers had large number of children and elders joined these centres. Subsequently, these centres used to provide significant income to the families of workers. However, in the last eight years, the network of these centres has broken down.That explains the least number of handicraft centres in the valley.

1.2. In the situation explained above which dominant numbe' of the handicraft workers work in their homes, the life-conditions in the government/private sponsored centres were not worse. The women workers in these centres get minimum required facilities in the summer and winter seasons. In response to our questions regarding the availability of non-economic facilities in these centres, while 70.00 per cent (i.e. 140 out of 200) respondents felt satisfied, 30.00 per cent (60 out of 200) respondents were not satisfied. These non-economic facilities included electricity, hygienic condition, heating arrangements and diet refreshments, Those women who felt satisfied belonged to the elder age groups, stayed for lesser time in the centres, and did some of their work: at their homes. On the other hand, 60 respondents who felt dissatisfied generally belonged to the younger age groups and spend comparatively more time in the centres. So, these centres have been reduced to the least number.

2. Work-input by the Workers

2.1. It is generally believed that the workers, working in all handicraft sectors at their homes or in out-home centres, usually get very less wages. These wages are completely disproportionate to their hard labour. In actuality, what they deserve for their hard, mannual and continuous work is denied to them. They are paid lesser wages in comparison to their male counterparts. Our investigation among the respondents revealed as is mentioned in the following table:

TABLE 2
WORK INPUT BY THE WOMEN WORKERS

S.No.	*Total Period*	*Actual Input Period*			
		C.W.	*P.M.*	*S.B.*	*P.S.B.N.*
1.	Hour per day	6.8	7.00	6.5	8.0

(Contd.)

(Contd. Table 2)

S.No.	*Total Period*	*Actual Input Period*			
		CW.	PM.	SB.	PSBN.
2.	Days per Week	5.3	5.8	6.0	6.0
3.	Days per Month	20.60	21.00	21.90	22.50
4.	Holidays per week	1.5	1.2	1.5	1.5

C.W - Carpet weaving

P.M.- Paper machie

S.B.- Shawl bafi

P.S.B.N. - Phum-Shahtosh-Blanket-Namda weaving.

The above statistical table clearly reveals that the women workers in general put maximum input in all handicraft sectors. Among the sample women in our study, they spent on an average 7.5 hours per day in the handicraft work. While in the P.S.B:N. areas, women workers spent 8 hours per day, in S.B. area they invested 6.5 hours per day. Second, women workers in our sample worked on an average 6 days per week. While dominant majority of respondents availed Friday as the off day, the minority of them availed Sunday as their weekly holiday. The women workers in the C.W. sector workers availed 5.3 days per week, while their counterparts in the P.S.B.N. sectors had six day per week record. Third, our respondents revealed that they usually worked 21 days per month. While workers in the P.M. sector worked 21 days in a month, the workers in the P.S.B.N. sectors invested 22.50 days a month. The work in the latter sector/s needs comparatively more work. Fourth, our investigation showed that the workers availed on an average 1.5 days per week as the weekly holiday. This pattern of holiday was similar in all handicraft sectors. As mentioned earlier, Friday is the most common weekly off-day among the women workers. Some among them go to the mosques for weekly prayers and visit the shrine.

2.2. The Table 2 reveals clearly that the nature of work is more or less same. It is highly labour intensive, demands maximum time input and has obselete technology. It is mannual, hard and continuous. Lesser work input cannot be afforded by the workers. Even majority of the workers availed minimum holidays. Some of them work even on holidays. The work in areas of phum-shahtosh weaving is more complex and costly relatively. In this field, while the women workers, mostly belonging to the upper age groups, spend more amount of money and earn more relatively. The other handicrafts demand less expenditure and lesser profits too.

2.3. Our investigation among the women workers in Kashmir regarding the average income and expenditure revealed the following:

TABLE 3
AVERAGE INCOME AND EXPENDITURE OF THE WOMEN WORKERS (PER MONTH)

S.No.	*Work Sector*	*Income*	*Expenditue*
1.	C.W.	940	70
2.	P.M.	925	90
3.	S.B.	870	100
4.	P.S.B.N.	896	170
	Average	907.75	107.50

The above reflects the meagre income of the workers in all areas. While the workers in C. W. and P.M. areas earn Rupees 940 - 925 per month, the workers in the areas of S.B. and P.S.B.N. earn Rupees 870 - 896 per month. At the same time, the resource expenditure of all workers is significant, taken into consideration their income level. While the first and second categories of workers spend Rupees 70 - 90, the third and fourth categories of workers spend Rupees 100 - 170 per month. Thus on an average, while a worker earns 901.75 rupees per month, she make an expenditure of 107.50 rupees per month. Taking into consideration the rising standard of life, nearly 100 per cent respondents felt that this was the meagre amount which will not suffice family needs. But, the women workers of younger age groups feel differently. It was because this amount was their personal income, while the family needs are fulfilled by the parents or elders.

3. Money Sufficient or not for Self/family needs

3.1. As is clear from the facts mentioned in the preceding section, the amount of money earned by the handicraft women worker not sufficient for their self and family needs. Though their material needs stand least comparatively, these are fulfilled partly, which provides the basis for their suffering in various fields of life. Our investigation among the sample of women workers in this regard divulges the facts mentioned in the following table:

TABLE 4
MONEY SUFFICIENT FOR SELF/FAMILY NEEDS OF THE WORKERS

S.No.	*Question*	*Response*				*No. Response*	
	Is the earned money	*Yes*	*No*				*No.*
	sufficient?	*No*	*%*	*No.*	*%*		
1.	-Self needs	120	60	45	22.5	35	17.5
2.	-Family needs	3	1.5	160	80	37	18.5

The above table statistics reveals that 60 per cent (i.e. 120 out of the total of 200) women worker respondents felt that their self needs were fulfilled even by the meagre income they earn in working in the handicraft-sectors. These respondents were members of very young age groups and their material needs were very limited and they belonged to lower income lowest in educated groups. These women respondents were mostly dependent on their families which fulfill their needs. On the other hand, 23 per cent respondents in our sample said that their self needs could not be fulfilled by the meagre income which they earn by working in the handicraft sectors. They belonged to the elder age groups and they spent money on the family needs keeping minimum amount for self use. Moreover, inflationery trends in the market make them more disadvantaged as their income has remained static for a long time.

3.2. With regard to the family needs, 1.5 per cent respondents in our sample revealed that these were fulfilled. This respose may be explained in terms of the respondents belonging to the lowest economic groups and their least economic needs. Their families had least number of members. On the other hand, 80.00 per cent (i.e. 160 out of 200) of our respondents felt that their family needs could not be fulfilled by their meagre income from the handicraft work they do. This dominant response is self revealing because the meagre income of the women workers can never match the rising cost standard of life. Our respondents revealed that this sub-standar life had necessary negative impact on their children's education, health, diet, personality growth and so on.

3.3. About 18 per cent (i.e. 36 out of 200) respondents gave no response. In fact, their response lie in between two extreme responses of 'yes' and 'no'. On the basis of our observation, we may say that these women's self and family needs were not fulfilled from the money which they earn from the handicraft work.

4. Utilization of Money Earned by Woman Workers

4.1. The amount of money which they get for their handicraft work is utilized by the women for different urposes related to their persons and families. There seem different patterns of the utilization of this money. This clearly reveals in the following table:

TABLE 5
PATTERNS OF UTILIZATION OF MONEY BY THE WOMEN WORKERS

S.No.	*Pattern of Response*	*Respondents number*	
		Number	*Percent*
1.	Handover to parents/ guardians	92	46
2.	Spend yourself for family needs	26	13
3.	Spend yourself for self needs	68	34
4.	Spend for other purposes	14	07
	Total	200	100

4.2. The above table reveals that 46 per cent (i.e. 92 out of 200) women worker respondents hand over the amount of income to their parents or guardians in their families. These respondents generally belong to the younger age groups and are completely dependent on their parents in economic as well as non-economic fields. In fact, all their needs are taken care of by their family heads. So, they are supposed to handover all their income to their parents. But, their parents don't spend this amount on their own or family needs. Generally, they spend it on the purchase of things needed at the time of marriage of the concerned girls. This type of income is considered "supportive income" to the family.

4.3. The above table also reveals that 34 per cent (i.e. 68 of 200) respondents spend the amont of money which they earn by working in the handicraft sectors) exclusively for self needs. These respondents mostly belong to very young age groups and are completely dependent on their families for fulfillment of their basic needs. They usually spent money for marriage related items such as golden ornaments, other jewellery things, clothes, crockery, cosmetics and so on. Their family don't demand money from them. It is because the parents get relief if their daughters take things for their marriage.

4.4.The table shows that 13 per cent (i.e. 26 out of 200) respondents of the sample spent the earned amount of money for family needs. These respondents were dependent on their families partly or wholly. That is why they had to take care of their family members' needs. Some of them had to spend for families basic needs. Some of them were widows who had the responsibility to take care of their entire families.

4.5. 7 per cent (i.e. 14 out of 200) of respondents the earned money for other purposes such as entertainment on particular occasions, gifts to friends, medical treatment, travel outside the state, buying a luxury item, and so on.

5. Family members of the workers

5.1. The general impression that women belonging to the lower classes/groups have larger number of children comparatively stands correct with regard to our working women respondents. In the context of these women, there emerges a corelation between lower economic status and larger number of children on an average. Thus our respondents maintain their joint families with larger number of children. Our enquiry in this regard revealed as mentioned in the following table:

TABLE 6
NUMBER OF FAMILY MEMBERS OF THE WORKERS

S.No.	*Earnings status*	*Number*	*Average*
1.	Non-Earning	1140	5.1
2.	Earning	660	3.3
	Total	1800	9.0

5.2.The above table reveals that all 200 of respondents had 1800 family members in total. It follows that a woman worker had about 9 family members on an average. This rate of family members (majority of whom are dependents) stands very high in comparison to the prevailing regional, national and international standards. But, this high rate may be explained in terms of the prevailing situation in the broader Indian society wherein the joint family with larger number of members is prevelant at large. Moreover, large number of family members in this situation is explained by saying that more members necessarily mean more earners and so more income. The table also reveals that while 660 members were earners, 1140 members were non-earners. It showed that there were more eaters than earners. The table shows that the woman worker had 5.7 non-earning and 3.3 earning members in the family on an average. It follows that each earning member had to feed two non-earning members. This reflects the hard economic conditions in their families.

5.3. These family members belonged to different age groups, which enabled them to contribute to their families differently. Our investigation about the age groups of members of families of the respondents revealed as is shown in the following table:

TABLE 7
AGE GROUPS OF FAMILY MEMBERS OF THE WORKERS

S.No.	*Age Groups*	*Number*	*Percentage*
1.	06-15 years	26	13
2.	16-2 years	60	30
3.	26-40 years	80	40
4.	40 above	34	17
	Total	200	100

5.4. The above table reveals that while the age groups of 26-40 and 40 above years constitute 57 per cent of the total number of families of women worker respondents, the age groups of 06-15 and 16-25 years number 43 per cent of the total. It follows that the elder age groups generally form the earning members in their families, while as the younger age groups are often non-earning members of their families. Both these Groups are mostly illiterate, but the latter group is also unemployed. Though the age group of 16-25 years stands most active and productive group, it is mostly dependent on the parental families.

5.5. Our investigation among the women workers showed that there prevailed general illiteracy among their family members. A significant degree among them have neither attended schools themselves nor their children go to the schools.Our investigation in this regard revealed as mentioned in the following table:

TABLE 8
EDUCATION AMONG THE MEMBERS OF FAMILIES OF THE WORKERS

S.No.	*Educated/Uneducated*	*Number*	*Per cent*
1.	Educated	60	30.00
2.	Uneducated	118	59.00
3.	No Response	22	11.00
	Total	200	100.00

5.6. The above statistical table reflects clearly the situation in which the dominant majority of the members of the women workers (59.00 per cent) are uneducated. This situation contributes as one of the crucial factors which forces the women at home to join the handicraft centres in their localities, even when they are relatively young.

6. Children of the Women Workers

6.1. As revealed in the previous section, the women workers in sample of respondents have large number of children on the whole. The explanation for this phenomenon has been provided in the preceding section. Our investigation in this regard gave us the informastion as mentioned in the Table 9.

TABLE 9
CHILDREN OF THE WOMEN WORKERS

S.No.	*Sex*	*School-Going Status*	*Number*	*Per cent*
1.	Boys	School Going	240	30.00
		Non-School Going	136	11.00
2.	Girls	School Going	304	38.00
		Non-School Going	120	15.00
3.	Total		800	100.00

6.2. The Table reveals that, out of the total number of 800 children of the women workers, the boys percentage is 41 per cent while girls constitute 53.00 per cent. Most of these boys and girls belong generally to age groups of below 15 years. Nearly all of them are dependent on their parents. The most important aspect of this situation is that the percentage of school-going girls is very significants. Same is more or less correct about the boys. Girls education is more crucial because they were not allowed to pursue education till few decades back. It follows that while the girls education is consistantly encouraged, there is very less resistance to their education. In this context, the above table of 800 children shows that, among boys, 30 per cent are school-going and 11 per cent are non-school going. On the other hand, among girls, 38 per cent are school going and 15 per cent are non-school going.

6.3. Our enquiry among the children of women workers also showed that while 58.00 per cent of the total children go to the government school, 42.00 per cent study in the private schools. As the fact stands, the government schools are cheapest but the quality of education is lowest. Moreover, the degree of responsibility and accountability is minimum in practice. On the other hand, the private schools are not cheap and the quality of education there is not so bad. Thus it follows that majority of the children of the women workers attend schools and get some degree of education. This the women workers afford with the help of other family members, especially husbands and brothers and sisters.

6.4. Regarding the classes of children, our investigation gave the following information:

TABLE 10
CLASS STATUS OF THE CHILDREN OF WOMEN WORKERS

S.No.	*Class*	*Number*	*Per cent*
1.	L.K.G		
	U.K.G.		
	First	368	46.00
2	II-V	320	40.00
3.	VI-IX	110	14.00
	Total.	800	100.00

6.5. The table shows that a significant number of children, i.e. 368 out of 800, are studying in the lowest classes of L.K.G., U.K.G. and First. Following this, 320 out of 800 children study in the classes of II to V. At the higher stage of VI to IX classes, 112 out of 800 children do study. The fact which reveals from this statistics is that there is a significant drop-out rate among children. This happens when the children go upwards to middle and higher-level classes.

7. Regularity in the Payment of Wages to Women Workers

7.1. As is the general practice, the women workers get handicraft work in different ways such as monthly wages and in lump sum. The nature of payment depends upon the nature of work and the time input. However, more important point is that whether.

These wages are paid to the workers regularly or not. It is because the regularity in paying the wages helps workers and non-regularity hurts the workers. Our investigation in this regard among the sample of women workers revealed the following statistics:

TABLE 11
REGULARITY IN THE PAYMENT OF WAGES TO THE WORKERS

S.No.	*Question*	*Response*						*No Response*	
		No		*Yes*					
		No.	*%*	*Theks*		*Lumpsum*		*No.*	*%*
				No.	*%*	*No.*	*%*		
1.	Do you get the wage regularly?	80	45	80	40	30	15	200	100

7.2. The above table tells that 45 per cent of the women/ worker respondents don't get their wages regularly, but 55 per cent of these respondents get their wages regularly (40 per cent on theka-basis and 15 per cent in lump sum). It follows that majority of the workers get their wages regularly because of economic and non-economic reasons. The economic reasons include (i) both parties are benefited in theka and lump sum types of payment. While the wholesalers/middlemen sends the material to the market in time, the workers dispose off their work in time. Thus both parties get more money and more profit, though proportionately, (ii) stronge economic motivation. On the other hand, the non-economic factors include the neighbourhood and other relations, which have a positive and strong impact on the payment of wages to the workers; helping attitude among the wholesalers/middlemen. This aspect 'has emerged crucial in the last several years of militancy.

7.3. On the other hand, a significant minority of 45 per cent don't maintain regularity in the payment of wages to the women workers. The reasons cited for this type of behavour by respondents included (i) non-availability of sufficient amount of money with the wholesalers/ middlemen at all times. While this argument is genuine some times, the wholesalers/middlemen use it to delay the payment sometimes. This is what has happened in the past several years of militancy; (ii) non-co-operative attitude and behaviour of the wholesalers/middlemen towards the workers; and delaying the payment of wages for months and years.

8. Suffering/Exploitation of Women Workers in Unorganized Sector

8.1.The general feeling prevails that the women workers in the unorganized sector suffer in many ways. While the working women in the organized sector get more wages comparatively and are entitled to economic and non-economic benefits, working women in the unorganized sector neither get just wages nor are entitled to any benefit. The latter also get exploited at the hands of the wholesalers and middle-men. During the investigation among the women workers, we asked a question in this regard. The response we got is included in the following table:

TABLE 12
SUFFERING OF THE WOMEN WORKERS

S.No.	*Question*	*Response*	
		Number	*Percent*
1.	Do you suffer more in comparison to the Women workers in organized sector?		
1.	Yes	140	70.00
2.	No	48	24.00
3.	No Response	12	6.00
	Total	200	100.00

8.2.The above table reveals clearly that 70.00 per cent dominant majority of women workers conveyed that they suffered in terms of least wages (that too paid very late) which could not be increased according to the market standards. It also divulged during the course of investigation that most of the women workers were not aware about the economic and other benefits, which the women workers in the organized sector get. The related fact is that the suffering of these women increase day by day. On the other hand, 24.00 per cent of respondents felt that they were not suffering by working in this field. These respondents were not totally dependent on this income for family needs. They belonged either to the elder or very young age groups. Most of these workers belonged to Shawl-bafi and shah-tosh handicraft sectors were the profit margin is more.

8.3. In this context, the general feeling prevalent among the women worker respondents was that they usually got exploited at the hands of the handicraft centres proprietors. Our inquiry in this connection got the following response:

TABLE 13
FEELINGS OF EXPLOITATION AMONG THE WORKERS

S.No.	*Question*	*Response*							
		Yes		*No*		*No Resp.*		*Total*	
		No.	*%*	*Yes*	*%*	*No.*	*%*	*No.*	*%*
1.	Are you economically exploited?	140	70	49	24	11	5.5	200	100

8.4. The above table reveals that while 70 per cent women respondents felt they were exploited, 24 per cent gave the opposite response. This type of response has maximum similarity with the type of response showed in the previous section. Moreover, the respondents said that about 80.00 per cent profits are grabbed by the wholesalers and middlemen.

8.5. Another related question was asked from the respondents, i.e.whether the prevailing exploitation can be stopped? In response, we got the following information:

TABLE 14
FEELINGS ABOUT STOPPAGE OF EXPLOITATION

S.No.	*Question*	*Response*							
		Yes		*No*		*No Resp.*		*Total*	
		No.	*%*	*Yes*	*%*	*No.*	*%*	*No.*	*%*
1.	Whether the exploitation can be stopped?	195	98	-	-	05	2	200	100

8.6. The Table 8.3 shows that over whelming majority of 98 per cenf respondents want and wish immediate stoppage of the ongoing exploitation. But, at the same time, they were not aware about how this exploitation can be stopped. This was mainly because they were not organized to fight against exploitation. The only alternafive respondents could think in this regard was the governmental intervention that may prove effective and durable.

9. Kowledge about organizations to Safeguard Interests

9.1. The important question emerges in the context of working conditions in the handicraft centres that when the women workers, get such meagre wages and get exploited at the hands of proprietors, wholesalers and middlemen, why they work in these centres/handicraft sector. We too felt in the same way. Though the women workers in sample worked very hard and for more time, they suffer in economic as well se non-economic fields. So, we asked this crucial question from the women respondents. Their unanimous, i.e., nearly 100 per cent, answer was that they had no other option except to adopt this occupation. So, they felt compelled to work in this field. They conveyed that most of them tried to get other, especially government jobs, but failed. Even after starting working *in* the handicraft field, they attempt continuously to get other jobs. It has been observed that when these women get other credible jobs, they shun this work immediately.

9.2 In the above context, the women workers suffer absolutely and get exploited. This type of suffering increases and intensifies in the absence of organizations/agencies which could have attempted to stop this suffering and exploitation of the women workers in the unorganized sector. So, in our investigation, we asked a pointed question to the respondents regarding the knowledge/working of an organization which is committed to -safeguard the interests of the women workers stop their exploitation. The response we got is recorded in the following table:

TABLE15
KNOWLEDE ABOUT ORGANIZATIONS IN UNORGANIZED SECTOR

S.No.	*Question*	*Response*							
		Yes		*No*		*No Resp.*		*Total*	
		No.	*%*	*Yes*	*%*	*No.*	*%*	*No.*	*%*
1.	Do you know any organnization working for your interests?	162	81	28	14	10	5	200	100

9.3. The above table reveals that 162 (81.00 per cent) respondents had the knowledge about functioning of organizations to safeguard their interests, while 28 (i.e. 14 per cent) respondents had no such knowledge. In actuality, no such organization existed in the unorganized sector of handicrafts. In comparison, many such organizations existed and functioned in the organized sectors. So, respondents felt that there was no individual or group or organization to safeguard their interests and stop exploitation. Consequently, they continue to suffer.

10. Impact on Health of Women Workers

10.1. The general impression which prevails among the people in Kashmir is that the continuous work in various handicraft sectors has adverse effect on the workers concerned. It has led to grave and acute health problems among the women workers especially backache, stomach disorder, mental problems and so on. Our observation in this regard confirmed these propositions. It also revealed that women of early-age groups and elder age groups become primary victims. This also reflected in the diet-intake pattern of the women workers in the centres during the day time. About 65.00 per cent respondents revealed that they do not get even the sufficient diet during time. In this context, we put a pointed question (do the continuous handicraft work affect your health adversely?) to the women respondents in this connection. The response we got is recorded in the following table:

TABLE 16
IMPACT ON HEALTH OF THE WOMEN WORKERS

S.No.	*Question*	*Response*					
	Do the continuous work affect your health adversely?	*Yes*		*No*		*Total*	
		No.	*%*	*No.*	*%*	*No.*	*%*
1.		120	60.00	80	40.00	200	100.00

10.2. The above response reveal that dominant majority felt that their health was affected adversely due to their continuous handicraft work, especially in the private centres where they neither get sufficient diet nor avail all necessary facilities. 60.00 per cent (i.e. 120 out of 200) respondents named the diseases, mentioned above) which developed among them primarily due to the continuous handicraft work. On the other hand, 80 (i.e. 40.00 per cent) respondents said that they were not (fully) affected by the continuous handicraft work. These respondents mostly worked at their homes where they got minimum required diet, entertainment and other necessary in-take items. However, these women too faced certain health problem but, these problems were not solely related to the continuous handicraft work by these women. In fact, there were other reasons which contributed to the rise of these diseases.

11. Social Estimation/Desirability of Handicraft Work by Women

11.1. As is the case wlth other occupations in the Kashmir valley, the handicraft related occupations are socially estimated/ evaluated. In general, these occupations, especially when women involved, are considered undesirable and are rated below in the ladder of occupations. In this context, were enquired from the women respondents in this regard. We got the response which is recorded in the table below:

TABLE 17
SOCIAL ESTIMATION OF THE HANDICRAFT WORK BY WOMEN

S.No.	*Positive/Negative Estimation*	*Resopnse*	
		Number	*Percent*
1.	They liked it	80	40.00
2.	They did not like it.	90	55.00
3.	No response	10	5.00
	Total	200	100.00

11.2. The above table reveals that while 80 (i.e. 40.00 per cent) respondents liked it, 110 (i.e. 55.00 per cent) respondents didn't like it. The reasons for the former type of response, which were cited by the respondents themselves, include it gives them certain level of income, engage the women, especially girls and elder women, during the day-time, and becomes the base for getting other jobs in other fields or in the government-sponsored centres.

These women generally belong to economically lower classes and lower occupational groups/communities. On the other hand, 110 (i.e. 55.00 per cent) respondents conveyed that they don't like this work but they were compelled to work in these sector primarily due to the economic needs. The rationale they provided for this response was that the handicraft work is generally attached to the inferior status which necessarily .affects their family image. This hurts them at the time of marriage and other important occasions.

11.3. In order to get deep response on the same theme, we asked questions from the respondents about the desirability/ undesirability of adopting the handicraft work by the women in their families. While 70.00 per cent respondents considered it desirable for their family members, the majority of 130 respondents felt it completely undesirable for their family members. The reasons they cited for their responses were more or less same as mentioned in the previous section. Continuing the theme, the respondents were asked whether they joined this occupation voluntarily or involuntarily. While o50 respondents said that they joined involuntarily, 50 upheld that they started this work voluntarily. The reasons for both types of responses were same as mentioned in the preceding sections.

12. The Role of Government vis-a-vis Women Workers

12.1. During the Course of our fieldwork the working women respondents put forward an argument repeatedly that they face a large number of problems and get exploited. In this situation, only the government can solve these problems and stop their exploitation. In this background, we asked a specific question regarding the government's help to these women. In reply to this question, the working women respondents gave the following response. 91.00 per cent of the respondetent sald that the government can provide them jobs in the handicraft centres, while 6.00 per cent respondents expected the government to provide them loans/monetary assistance for starting their own centres. Other respondents revealed that the government can provide them jobs in any office.

13.Various Problems of the Women Workers

13.1. The respondents in this study faced numerous problems. In this regard, we asked them to mention these problems, which are as follows (excluding those which have been mentioned in different sections):

- irregular and least wages,
- least profits to the women workers;
- shortage of raw material;
- exploitative role of the centre proprietors;
- emotional disturbance;
- laziness and tiredness;
- laborious occupation;
- suffering of the household jobs;
- various health problems;
- people don't like this occupation.

Suggestions

1. Establishment of the Co-operatives

Many of the basic and crucial problems faced by the working women (WW). In the unorganized handicraft sector may be solved, partly or wholly, by !he establishment and efficient-effective functioning of the co-operatives (CO) in the rural as well as urban areas. Though these COPs may be established by the government or at the initiation of the government, their efficient and effective functioning depends on the full participation of the concerned women individuals and women organizations. The structure of these co-operatives will represent governmental and non-governmental individuals, agencies and organizations. Taking into consideration the overall scenario of the WW in unorganised sector, these COPs may take care *of* the following needs

(i) to provide the basic infrastructure, especially the raw material, to the needy regularly and throughout the year at the minimum possible rates;

(ii) to purchase various kinds of products produced 'by the WW throughout the year and pay them the maximum possible rates;

(iii) to establish the network of outlets at the local, regional and international levels in terms of establishing/organizing melas, exhibitions, emporiums, wholesale and retail shops;

(iv) In addition to these formal initiatives and efforts, the COPs may prove highly relevant and effective in making the WW and working girls conscious about various issues and problems, especially attainment of literacy savings, fixation of due wages to the WW, demand of due and just rights, in the bank, and improvement of their life conditions.

2. Due Wages to the Women Workers

In actuality, there prevails no set standard or criteria of the wages paid to the WW for their work. So, the crucial and immediate need emerges for the fixation of wages for different HC items. These wages can be fixed on the prices basis, per inch-feet basis, per--item basis and so on. The important point here is that the existing wages have to be increased to the maximum satisfaction of the WW.

The government has to play an active role in this regard. Moreover, the regularity of the payment of all wages at the end of every month or any specific period agreed by the parties concerned must be ensured. The failure in maintaining this practice must be made an offence and punishable by law.

3. Stopping of the Exploitation of the WW

In order to stop the ongoing exploitation of the WW effectively and in as less time as possible, certain important actions have to be initiated by the non-governmental and governmental agencies/organizations. The first step in this direction is to fix the wages of the WW for the HC articles which they produce by their hands. The second step in this direction is to minimize/eliminate/negate the exploitative role of the middlemen in the HC sector. This may be done by debasing the basis of exploitation through the functioning of the HC cooperatives which will provide the necessary raw to the WW, buy the things produced by them and sell these things in the national and international markets through their network of outlets. The exploitative role of the wholesalers in the HC sector can also be minimized by the formal legislation in the field. In addition, the existing workload of WW has to be lessened significantly. The work-input of the WW has to be related with the wage-cost output. In regard to all these aspects, the government has to take necessary actions in terms of framing the relevant laws and rules and implementing these strictly.

4. Change in the Conditions of HC Centres

The existing conditions in the governmental as well as in non-governmental centres need to be changed radically for the betterment of the WW in various HC centres. In the government-sponsored and government-controlled HC centres, all material and non-material facilities such as enough space, hygienic conditions clean environment, and sufficient-regular diet during the day time. On the other hand, privately-owned and privately-controlled HC centres must also ensure such basic facilities. Moreover these centres must also pay the wages to the WW in full, regularly and according to the standard rates. The most important aspect about these facilities in both types of HC centres is that there must be strict, regular .and effective monitoring by the governmental agencies. The centres which deviate or violate the standard practices and norms must be punished as per the laws and rules framed and enacted in this regard.

5. Literacy of the WW and Children

One of the crucial implications of the continuous HC work carried out in both types of centres by the WW is that they (and their children too) remain illiterate/ uneducated. In significant number of cases, it leads to the drop-outs in the school at the earlier stages of formal education. This trend has to be checked and finally stopped through formal and non-formal measures. In this regard, a minimum degree of literacy/education has to be necessarily imparted to the WW in all types of HC centres. While the governmental HC centres can provide the facilities because these centres have lified and train teacher/s), the privately-owned centres have no such facility. But, the latter must also develop this facility with the support of the government. Continuous monitoring of this facility and recording of the immediate results must be those centre found violating or deviating from the standard practices must be punished seriously.

In the operational framework, these literacy/educational programmes, especially in terms of holding classes, can be carried out for half a day or less than thats but not less than two hours a day. It seems necessary to mention here that these literacy/ educational facilities must be provided to the WW and their children of earlier age groups.

6. To Negate the participation of Girl Child Labour (GCL)

The generally accepted principle that the child labour, particularly the GCL, must be discouraged, should be upheld and adhered to. This needs certain specific measures on the part of the government, HC centres and WW. First, the WW in the HC centres must not be allowed to take their children, especially girls, for the HC work neither in the centres nor in their own homes. Second, if GCL cannot avoid working for financial and poor family considerations, they must be provided necessary formal and technical education. Subsequently, the govt. must help them in developing careers in their relevant fields. Third the GCLs .must be provided necessary financial support, especially scholarships and stipends, for the education and training.

7. Improvement in the Conditions of the HCCs

In the context of the WW in unorganised sector in Kashmir, there emerges an absolute and urgent need to improve the pathetic conditions prevailing in the HC centres, especially the privately-owned centres. These conditions include payment of due wages regularly, availability of various raw-materials; providing proper diet during working hours/making arrangements for hygienic, soft environmental and cleaner conditions; provision for holidays and entertainment; carrying out health check ups regularly, and so on. All these and other measures have to be carried out at the official and non-official levels. While the governmental agencies and organizations will arrange for conditions requiring full monitary support, the non-governmental agencies and centres will take care of all other facilities. In this way, the service and life conditions of the WW may be improved significantly.

8. Initiation of the Social Legislation

Taking into consideration the safeguard of basic rights-interests and solution of the problems of the WW in HCCs, the process of formulation of social legislation in the relevant areas has to be started by the government. The implementation to be done by the governmental agencies and organizations will also lead to desirable change and improvement in the overall life conditions of the WW. The legislation may deal with social, economic, health, educational, environmental, psychological and other necessary fields of the life of WW.

9. Involvement of the NGOs

In addition to the role of the government, the multi-dimensional role of the NGOs must be involved and utilized fully for two specific reasons. First, it will lead to the successful operanationalization / implementation of the programmes aimed at the overall welfare of the WW and their families. Second it will lead to the realistic and immediate solution of all existing/emerging problems which hurt their life. Moreover, the effective role of the NGOs vis-a-vis HCs will take care of all these problems which the governmental agencies and organizations cannot solve. Special mention may be made of the psychological problems of the WW and low social estimation of the work performed by the WW and its immediate negative impact throughout their life-span, especially at the time of their marriage. Moreover, special efforts may be carried out by the NGOs to raise the consciousness among the WW and others about spending their earned money on themselves rather than handing it over to senior household member.

10. Adoption of New Technolony

For efficient functioning of and quality production by the HCCs , the old and obselete technology in all HC centres has to be necessarily replaced by modern technology at all stages and in all sub-sectors. Both, the GOs and NGOs, have to work in this direction. While the government has to provide the financial support for the purchase of new technology, the NGOs and HCCs have to make arrangement for adjustment of WW in new technology and to develope relevant attitude and work culture among the WW.

11. Arrangement for Heath Care

The health problems of the WW in the HCCs emerge as one of the crucial areas which deserves governmental as well as non-governmental attention. Work at two levels need to be done in this regard. First, all necessary preventive care must be taken by the administrators of the members in HCCs, so that they do not fall prey to the health hazards. Second, the government make it obligatory to make health check-up of the WW due to the work in HCCs, these must be cured properly. Moreover, administrators must be warned against not paying proper attention to the emerging health problem among the WW.

12. WW in the Homes

All above points must be applied to the WW who work in their own homes in ones, twos or threes. Proper attention must be given to their rights, interests and problems.

Appendix

D/T/W ____________
No. ____________

A. Background Information

A.1. Name/Caste

A.2. H. O. F./ Relation with HOF

A.3. Age Group
- 11-20 years
- 21-35 years
- 36-50 years
- 51 and above

A.4. Marital Status
- married
- unmarried
- divorced
- separated
- widow
- any other category

A.5. Income group
- less than Rs. 2000 [p.m.]
- Rs. 2001-4000
- Rs. 4001-6000
- Rs. 6001-8000
- Rs. 8001-10000
- Rs. 10000 and above

A.6. Literate — Yes/No
- if yes, educational qualification

A.7. Religion
- Hindu
- Muslim
- Sikh
- Christian
- Bodh
- any other religion

A. 8. Occupation
- self
- family

A. 9. Type of family you live in
- nuclear
- joint

No. of family members
- Total
- male
- female
- major
- minor
- earning
- not earning

A.10. Name of mother-tongue ____________________

Other languages know ____________________

____

A.11. Place of residence

- Rural area
  - Village ____________________
  - BlockfTehsil ____________________
- Urban area
  - Mohalla ____________________
  - Block/Tehsil ____________________
  - Previous ____________________
  - Present ____________________

B. Social Problems

B.1. Is the practice of dowry in vogue in your

- family yes/no
- clan yes/no
- community yes/no
- area yes/no

- if it is in amount, how much ______
- if it is in things, major items ______

______

______

B.2. How much amount of *mahr* was fixed at the time of marriage

______

- was it paid fully at that time yes/no
- if no, how much amount was paid ______
- how much amount is still unpaid ______

B.3. Are you the first only wife of your husband yes/no

- if no, how many wives he has - 02
  - 03
  - 04
- where other wife/wives live ______
- what problems you face due to your husband's marriage with more than one woman ______

______

______

B.4. Have you been divorced ever yes/no

- if yes, what was/were the reasons ______

______

have you remarried ______

- if yes, who took the care of children ______

______

____

____

- if no, has it occurred in your family/locality yes/no
- if yes, how many in last 1 year ____________________

B.5. After the marriage, were you given your share of parental property yes/no

- if yes, how much [% of your share]
- if no, reason/s ____________________________

____

____

B.6. After the marriage, how were your marital/social relations in the in-law family

relations with	good/better/best	bad/worse/worst
- husband	________	________
- father-in-law	________	________
- mother-in-law	________	________
- sister-in-law	________	________
- others	________	________

- if bad, were you beaten by your husband yes/no

B.7. If you are a working woman,

- where do you work ____________________
- has his work given rise to your duel role yes/no
- how you manage it ____________________

B.8. Since you remain out of your house for most time of the day, who takes care of your children.

- husband's family
- parents family
- servant/maid
- other relatives

- any other person
- how does it affects the socialization of the child
  - positive
  - negative
- does it lead to -deviance among children yes/no
- social control of family yes/no
- other problems ______________________

____

____

____

B.9. Since you remain out of your home on all working days, how it affects.

- your relations with your husband______________________
- your relations with in-laws______________________
- your relations with near/distant relatives______________________

____

____

C. Economic Problems

C.1. What was/is the occupation of your parental family________

- has it been changed yes/no
- if no, cite reason________
- if yes, what is the new occupation________

C.2. Do you work on land in your village yes/no

- if yes, on your own land
  , on other land
- if yes, do you get wages for the work yes/no
  , are these wages sufficient yes/no
  , if not, why ________

C.3. Do you work on handicrafts at your home yes/no

- if yes, what h.c. Items you work on________

, do you get due wages for your work yes/no

- if no, why ________
- if yes, does this fulfil your needs yes/no
- do you feel you are exploited yes/no
- if yes, give rationale ________

C.4. Are you working in the governmental/non-governmental office. Yes/no

if yes, where is your office located - in your area
- other area

, how much regular salary you get per month Rs.............

,does it gives you economic independence yes/no
,do you hand over salary to - in-laws
- keep with you
,do you spend it yourself yes/no
,do you spend it for - self needs
- family needs

C.5. What type of economic activity you performed in your area in the last year
- Rural area ______________________________
____
- Urban area ______________________________
____
- did this activity gave you wages yes/no
- if yes, were these wages sufficient yes/no
- cite reasons ______________________________
____

C.6. Do you feel that educated women must necessarily get govt. jobs yes/no
- reason/s ______________________________
____
____

C.7. Have you been benefited economically by the govt. programmes yes/no
- if yes, name the progs. ______________________________
____
____

C.8. What was the effect of your economic condition on
- marriage ______________________________
- migration ______________________________
- social status ______________________________
____

D. Educational Problems

D.1. Are you a literate person yes/no
if yes, qualification ____________________
if no, reason/s ____________________
____
____

D.2. Who are the educated persons in your

parental family	Husband's family
- father	- father
- mother	- mother
- brother/s	- brother/s
- sister/s	- sister/s
- near relative	- near relative

D.3. Family education chart:
- Total number of family members ____________________

- No. of educated - male ____________________
- female ____________________

- No. of uneducated - male ____________________
- female ____________________

- Nature of education - general - primary ____________________
- secondary ____________________
- higher ____________________
- college ____________________
- university ____________________

- Place of education - within the JK state ____________________
- Outside the J K state ____________________
- within India ____________________
- outside India ____________________

D.4. Are the educational facilities available to your child/children satisfactory yes/no

- if yes how many schools/institutions are in your
  - village/mohalla ____________________
  - block ____________________
  - tehsil ____________________
- if no,how many schools/institutions you need in
  - village/mohalla ____________________
  - block ____________________
  - tehsil ____________________

D.5. Total no. of school-going children in your family

Total ____________________
male ____________________
female ____________________

- how many of them dropped Total ____________________
  male __________ stage __________
  female __________ stage __________
- major reson/s for drop-out ____________________

____

____

- could it had been avoided yes/no
- if yes, how ____________________

____

____

D.6. What is the total cost of education on your school-going children

per month ____________________
per year ____________________

D.7. Do your children go to - government schools ____________________
- private schools ____________________

- reasons ____________________

____

D. 8. Do you feel that your children education stands career-oriented yes/no

- if yes, which career they may develop ________________

____

____

D. 9. What is the medium of instruction in the school/s of your children

- English
- Urdu
- Hindi
- Kashmiri
- Any other

E. Health Problems

E. 1. What kind of health facilities are available in your area

Facility	Rural	Urban
- Governmental		
- D./SD. Hospital	________	________
- P.H.C.	________	________
- Any other	________	________
- Non-governemental		
- Nursing homes	________	________
- H. Centres	________	________
- Drug shops	________	________
- Clinical Lab.	________	________
- Any other	________	________

E. 2. Have your children undergone Immunization course fully

yes/no

- if yes, have they got
  - BCG
  - DPT
  - Polio
  - Measles
  - Others
- if no, reasons ________

____

____

E.3. Which diseases are common in your area [rate-wise]

____

____

____

____

- how can these be stopped ______________________________

____

____

E. 4. Have you/your family member taken pre-natal and post-natal care during the last pregnancy yes/no

- if yes, where
  - PHC
  - PHC
  - PNH
  - AO
- Who conducted your/your family member's last delivery
  - Doctor
  - ANM
  - Trained dai
  - Untrained dai
  - Relative
  - Neighbour
  - AO person
- Where the last delivery took place
  - Hospital
  - PNH
  - Home
  - AO Place

E.5. Number of children surviving

	gave birth	living	died
- total	________	________	________
- male	________	________	________
- female	________	________	________

- Do you want more children yes/no

- if yes, how many - Total
  - Male
  - Female

- Has more number of children affected your health yes/no
- if yes, how ____________________

E.6. When you fall ill, what you do at that time
- go to the priest
- go to the drugs shop
- go to the PHC
- go to the expert doctor
- any other action ____________________

E.7. How many times you have visited the local PHC
- in last one month
- in last one year
- What services were offered there ____________________

____

____

E.8. Do you breast feed your child/children yes/no
- if no, reasons ____________________

____

____

E.9. Are you aware about family planning programmes yes/no
- if no, reasons ____________________

____

____

- if yes, which method you have opted
  - IUD/cut
  - Oral pills
  - Condom
  - Any other

F. Discrimination Problems

F.1. If you are working women, are you harassed at your place of work yes/no

- if yes, by whom ____________________

____

- nature of harassment ____________________

____

- have you complained against it yes/no
- if yes, result ____________________

____

- if no reason/s ____________________

____

F.2. If you are working in govt./non-govt. organization/ office, are you paid lesser wages than men yes/no

- if yes, how much % less
- , have you complained against it yes/no
- , any result ____________________

____

F. 3. If you work at home [for earning money], do you deal with handicraft items yes/no

- if yes, what h.c. items your work on ____________________

____

____

- do you get equal [to you men] wages yes/no
- if no, reason/s ____________________

____

- if you do other kinds of work yes/no
- if no, reason/s ____________________

____

F. 4. Do you feel that women is discriminated in inheritance rights existing in our law/society yes/no

- if yes, give rationale ______________________

____

F.5. Do religion become a base for discrimination against women yes/no

- if yes, explain ______________________

____

____

F.6. Do you feel that certain laws go against women's interest yes/no

- if yes, cite the laws ______________________

____

____

F. 7. Who holds the authority/control vis-a-vis

- property man/woman
- daily decisions man/woman
- marriage man/woman
- money investment man/woman
- children's education man/woman
- construcation of new house man/woman

F.8. How are women discriminated

In-family situation	out-family situation
______________________	______________________
______________________	______________________
______________________	______________________
______________________	______________________

F. 9. Do you feel that the girl child is discriminated in comparison to the boy child yes/no

- if yes, how ____________________

____

____

- if no, rationale ____________________

____

____

F.10. Why women go for abortion of female foetus

____

____

____

Index